INSIGHT AND ACTION

How to Discover and Support a Life of Integrity and Commitment to Change

va Green and Peter Woodrow
with Fran Peavey

New Society Publishers
Philadelphia, PA   Gabriola Island, BC

Library of Congress Cataloging-in-Publication Data

Green, Tova.
  Insight and action : how to discover and support a life of integrity and commitment
  to change / by Tova Green and Peter Woodrow, with Fran Peavey.
    p. cm.
  Includes bibliographical references.
  ISBN 0-86571-296-4. ISBN 0-86571-295-6.
  1. Small groups.   2. Self-help groups.   3. Community development.   4. Social
  change.   I. Woodrow, Peter.   II. Peavey, Fran.   III. Title.
HM133.G7   1994   302.3'4--dc20   94-10242

Inquiries regarding requests to reprint all or part of *Insight and Action: How to Discover
and Support a Life of Integrity and Commitment to Change* should be addressed to New
Society Publishers, 4527 Springfield Avenue, Philadelphia, PA, 19143.

| ISBN Hardcover | USA 0-86571-295-6 | CAN 1-55092-246-7 |
| ISBN Paperback | USA 0-86571-296-4 | CAN 1-55092-247-5 |

Cover design by Laura Joyce Shaw. Book design by Martin Kelley. Printed on partially-
recycled paper using soy-based ink by Capital City Press of Montpelier, Vermont, USA.

To order directly from the publisher, add $2.50 to the price for the first copy, and add
75¢ for each additional copy. Send check or money order to:
  In the United States: *In Canada:*
  New Society Publishers   New Society Publishers
  4527 Springfield Avenue   PO Box 189
  Philadelphia, PA 19143   Gabriola Island, BC VOR 1XO

New Society Publishers is a project of the New Society Educational Foundation, a
nonprofit, tax-exempt, public foundation in the United States, and of the Catalyst
Education Society, a nonprofit society in Canada. Opinions expressed in this book do
not necessarily represent positions of the New Society Educational Foundation, nor the
Catalyst Education Society.

TABLE OF CONTENTS

FOREWORD:
FACTS ABOUT GEESE*

Milton Olsen (the Naturalist) said it's very interesting that, particularly with geese, we have a lot to learn about collectives.

Fact One: As each bird flaps its wings, it creates an uplift for the birds following it. By flying in a V-formation, the whole flock adds 71 percent greater flying range than if the bird flew alone. Many indigenous cultures recognize that there's a lot I can do by myself, there's a lot I can do with a partner, but the power of what I can get done with a collective is quantum. It's a mega-step, it's a mega movement. The lesson from this fact: people who share a common direction and sense of community can get where they're going quicker and easier because they're traveling on the thrust of one another. That's a universal collective lesson.

Fact Number Two About Geese: Whenever a goose falls out of formation it suddenly feels the drag and resistance of trying to fly alone and quickly gets back into formation to take advantage of the lifting power of the bird immediately in front. Lesson: If we have as much sense as a goose, we will stay in formation with those who are headed where we want to go and be willing to accept their help, as well as give ours to others.

Fact Number Three: When the lead goose gets tired, it rotates back into the formation and another goose flies at the point position. An invaluable lesson for us to apply to all group work. It pays to take turns doing the hard tasks and sharing leadership. With people as with geese, we are interdependent on each others' skills and capabilities and unique arrangements of gifts, talents, resources, or what indigenous societies call the "good, true, and beautiful."

---

*From a talk by Angeles Arrien to the Organization Development Network, 1992.

Fact Number Four: The geese in formation honk from behind to encourage those in front to keep up their speed. Lesson: we need to make sure our honking from behind is encouraging. And not something else. In groups where there is greater encouragement against great odds, the production is much greater — the power of encouragement. Now, I love the word courage because it means "to stand by one's heart, to stand by one's core." To encourage someone else's core, to encourage someone else's heart—*that* quality of honking.

Fact Number Five: When a goose gets sick, or wounded, or shot down, two geese drop out of formation and follow it down to help and protect it. They stay with it until it is able to fly again or dies. Then they launch out on their own with another formation or catch up with the flock. Lesson: if we have as much sense as geese, we too will stand by each other in difficult times as well as when we are strong. And I think it's important that one of the things indigenous cultures have done for years is that they look to nature as an outer mirror of one's own internal nature. And so as we begin to learn about collectives of animals and their patterns, perhaps we have some tools, techniques, methodologies about community and about collective work and group work.

INTRODUCTION

You are not alone. You don't have to make the most important decisions in your life by yourself. Together, we have resources around us to sustain us in our difficult work to make the world more just, safe, and sustainable for all.

> *"I feel drawn towards work against violence in the schools. It's going to be emotionally demanding and physically threatening work. Will you support me as I get into this? Are there ways I can support you in your work?"*

> *"I think my path is taking me towards using my artistic talents to stimulate new ways of thinking about the relationships between women and men. This would be a major career change for me. Would you help me think through this decision?"*

> *"I want to develop new ways to run socially-responsible businesses that don't exploit people or the environment. Can you help me keep on track with this work?"*

The authors have given this book the title *Insight and Action*. We gain *insight* as we search within ourselves for greater self-understanding, for the seeds of growth and change, for inklings about the right path for us. We take *action* as we set out upon that path, absorbing the experiences we find there, noticing how they change us, gathering new insights about ourselves and the world around us.

Work for change is a constantly evolving process. When we act, we can learn. If we pay attention, action generates insights, from which flow ideas for more accurate and effective action. Action can also lead to periods when we need to reflect, to rededicate, or to redirect our energies. In order to sustain our work for a better world, to make it increasingly effective, we need support, compassionate critique, and challenging perspectives.

Insight and Action is about how we can sustain our commitments to creating the kind of world in which we want to live. All of us involved in such work have moments of doubt, indecision, frustration, and/or discouragement. The main message of this book is that we don't have to tough it out alone at such moments; we can get help from people in our communities—our friends, fellow workers, members of our religious groups, and relatives.

This book provides guidelines for making decisions, and for organizing support and accountability in our work for the world. It presents three processes:

> *Support Groups* which provide ongoing, regular and mutual encouragment and challenge from friends or colleagues;
>
> *Clearness Groups* which offer focused attention to individuals who are facing important decisions and assist them in discovering their own wisdom and integrity;
>
> *Strategic Questioning* which promotes deep reflection and change, and helps uncover actions, dreams, and strategies buried under fear and helplessness.

These three modes have each survived the test of time. They have been used by people all over the United States and in other countries. The three processes can be used in a variety of circumstances and in numerous combinations.

How the Three Processes Interact

The issues of commitment to action and personal growth encouraged through support groups can be brought, at important decision points, to a clearness group, especially when the time devoted to any single person in a support group is too limited for full consideration of all issues. A one time (or two time) clearness meeting can also involve additional people beyond the support group—from a person's workplace, faith community, or other friends. (Of course, it is not necessary to be in a support group to hold a clearness session!)

> *Teri had been a member of The Gang support group for about a year when she was told she might lose her job. She was questioning many things, including whether she and her family would continue to live in the Bay Area or move to a smaller town. After talking about her questions during her time in a meeting of The Gang, she decided to hold a clearness session, including some members of the support group, plus family and friends.*

The kind of focused attention of a clearness meeting can be developed in an ongoing way through a support group. While a clearness committee is meant to provide help only at a significant decision point, a support group offers sustained assistance over time.

Pat and his partner had a wonderful experience with a clearness process; they decided to go ahead and have a child, even though it meant that each of them would make career sacrifices. Now, with parenthood impending, Pat was terrified about how to be a father and maintain his commitments to a social change career. He decided to form a support group with other new fathers he knew through his activist work.

Strategic Questioning is a communication and thinking discipline which will bring zest, creative energy, and sometimes surprising strategies for action to support groups, clearness meetings, and many other social change endeavors.

Robin had been stewing in the support group for weeks and expressing her outrage. She kept worrying at the issue of "why don't people in my organization see the racism in their hiring processes? They talk about affirmative action, but the same middle-class white people keep getting hired. I want to understand the system here!" Dale finally asked, "Robin, what would it take for you to play a powerful force for change on this issue in the organization?" Ashley added, "What will it look like on the other side of the changes you want? How might the organization get there?"

These three processes are all about people, the way that we think, feel, and act, individually and in groups or organizations. Every group of people is more than the sum of its parts and the authors hope that this book is more than simply a sum of its three distinct but interconnected parts.

How This Book Came to Be Written

An earlier version of the section on support groups originally appeared as *Keeping Us Going*, a joint publication by Interhelp and Movement for a New Society (MNS) in 1986. That manual was a collaborative writing effort by Sarah Conn, Tova Green, Nancy Moorehead, Anne Slepian, and Peter Woodrow, all from the Boston area at the time. It was photocopied and distributed mainly through the Despair and Empowerment Workshops led by Joanna Macy and the Interhelp network. Anne Slepian and Christopher Mogil encouraged Tova to expand and update the manual.

A manual on clearness processes was written by Peter Woodrow and published by Movement for a New Society in 1976 as *Clearness: Processes for Supporting Individuals and Groups in Decision-Making*, mainly for use within MNS groups, collectives, and cooperative households. In the years since then, the clearness process has gained interest in a number of quarters. Some social change communities use it actively. Many Quaker groups have revived and expanded its use for spiritual discernment. Several Catholic religious orders have adapted the clearness process as a part of their community life as well. Section II of this book is a revision of the earlier manual and addresses both social change activists and religious communities—and leaves room for many other adaptations, limited only by human inventiveness.

The Strategic Questioning section is the latest account of the ideas and skills which Fran Peavey has been developing for many years. Students from Strategic Questioning workshops which Fran has led in Australia, India, New Zealand, and the United States have contributed to her work in this area. The section on Strategic Questioning also appears in Fran Peavey's book, *By Life's Grace* (New Society Publishers, 1994).

We welcome comments and stories from readers about how support groups, clearness meetings, and strategic questioning make a difference in your work and life. Please write to any of us care of New Society Publishers.

Acknowledgments

Tova Green writes: This book was written with the support of many people! I wish to thank Anne Slepian and Christopher Mogil for encouraging me to revise the manual *Keeping Us Going*. Fran Peavey made many contributions to the book, through both her writing and her loving support. Everyone in my support group, The Gang, took an interest in this project. Special thanks to Fran Peavey, Rita Archibald, and Berne Weiss for vignettes, to Bev Ramsey for the group photo, to Carole Schein, Carol Rothman, Rita Archibald, and Berne Weiss for reading parts of the first draft (and to Nicole Milner), and to Amy Mar for making a tape of a meeting of her East Coast support group. Thanks to members of Amy's East Coast group, Jane Klassen from Ahimsa in Seattle, and Nicholas Herold of the Papa's group in Boston for contributing vignettes. Thanks also to Joanne Sunshower of Interhelp for her interest and support.

Peter Woodrow writes: I appreciate the persistence of New Society Publishers for continuing to print the earlier "Clearness Manual," a small work which had a steady audience, but which earned them very little money! In preparing the present version, I have been inspired by the work of Jan Hoffman, Parker Palmer, and Patricia Loring who have continued to develop the clearness process, particularly among Quakers. Thanks to Steve Chase, Jan Hoffman and Mary Link for reviewing the draft manuscript and to Hugh Barbour for information on Quaker history. Jan, Mary and David Foster provided a wonderful resource by gathering materials on clearness over the years, several of which are reproduced in this volume. Thanks to Jan Hoffman, Jan Wood, and Quaker Hill Conference Center for giving permission to reprint their materials.

Fran Peavey writes: Many people have contributed to the development and organization of the social technology of Strategic Questioning. Vivian

Hutchinson, Rita Archibald, Carol Perry, Stuart Anderson, Cath Fisher and Barbara Hirshkowitz have made special contributions.

We have enjoyed collaborating on this project—by phone, fax, and express mail. We have all found Barbara Hirshkowitz at New Society Publishers an interested, informed, and enthusiastic editor.

Tova Green
Oakland, California

Fran Peavey
San Francisco, California

Peter Woodrow
Cambridge, Massachusetts

January 1994

Section I

SUPPORT GROUPS

by Tova Green

INTRODUCTION

In March 1982 after I emerged from a weekend Despair and Empowerment workshop with Joanna Macy, I was determined to sustain my passion to do something to stop the proliferation of nuclear missiles. I knew I couldn't do it alone, and sensed that joining an organization would not be enough. A neighbor, Mica, whom I didn't know very well, was also in the workshop. I asked her if she would be interested in forming a support group. She said yes and we decided to invite Mona, who lived in my building. Mona hadn't been to the workshop, but I knew from many conversations with her that she was concerned about world events.

We began meeting every two weeks in the morning, with tea and muffins, rotating apartments. During that year Mona attended a Despair and Empowerment workshop. She began to think of doing her Ph.D. dissertation on activists who sustained their commitment. I checked out several local peace groups, looking for a group whose style and goals were in harmony with my own. Then I attended a second Despair and Empowerment workshop, and decided to deepen my involvement with Joanna Macy's network, Interhelp. I attended a training to lead Despair and Empowerment workshops and a national meeting of the organization, where I met many people from different parts of the U.S. In the course of the year Mica decided to leave her catering job and join the staff of a large meditation center near Boston.

Mica left the group and Mona and I invited others to join us. Our group lasted for five years. At its largest we were five: Mona, Suzy, Chris, Gavin and I. We were all involved in Interhelp; otherwise our lives were very different. Mona was commuting to New York every week to work on her Ph.D. in psychology and worked part time as a psychologist. Chris worked for a coalition of peace groups, of which he became director. Gavin had a strong commitment to meditation and worked as an accountant. Suzy, who had teen-age children, returned to work as a fund raiser for a peace organization. I had a psychotherapy and consulting practice. We differed in age, gender, sexual preference, religion, and class background.

We maintained the every two weeks, tea and muffins routine. We helped one another through many changes in our work and our personal lives, and came to love one another. We always started with a "check-in," a brief update about each of our lives, then divided the time equally. Each of us could ask for whatever we wanted in our time—help with goal setting, feedback on an idea, emotional support, encouragement to take a risk. We seldom did projects together, but encouraged each other's individual directions. After an overnight retreat at a friend's house on Cape Cod, we did organize a fundraiser for Interhelp, a "Slumber for Peace" party. We provided a campfire and singing, overnight accommodation and Sunday brunch. It was fun and financially successful.

During this period I began traveling to do Interhelp workshops in Canada and Europe. At the end of one workshop I emerged with a goal that surprised me: to do Despair and Empowerment workshops in Japan. It took me a year to achieve that goal. My support group helped in many ways, both emotionally and concretely. I had never been to Japan and knew only one person there, but I had been drawn to Japanese movies, art, literature. I wanted to visit Hiroshima and Nagasaki and meet people in the Japanese peace movement. I wondered if there were feminists in Japan and what life was like for them in such a patriarchal society. The support group helped me combat self-doubt; draw a time line of what I would have to do in order to go; write a fund-raising letter; and make a flyer to send to groups in Japan who might sponsor workshops or talks. By the time I left I had a full itinerary of talks, workshops, and meetings with peace groups and women's groups and had raised all the money I needed.

After moving to California I joined a support group that has been meeting since the early 1980s. The group now consists of ten women and meets once a month on a Sunday morning. This group helped me begin to feel at home in a new city and to make connections with other activists. During the Gulf War it reminded me that I was not alone with my despair and concern. It has also helped with several projects I have undertaken, including the writing of the first section of this book.

Now it is hard for me to imagine being politically active without a support group. One thing that has given me hope over the last decade has been knowing that I, and my support group, are part of a vast international web of people who care deeply about life and our planet. Together we can do what none of us can do alone.

Is a Support Group for You?

Perhaps my story reminded you of some of your own experiences. Are you a social change worker with any of the following problems or struggles?

Time management

Despair/hopelessness

Developing or improving personal leadership

Getting motivated to do important reading/studying

Avoiding "burnout" or overcommitment

Dealing with conflicts with fellow activists

Choosing priorities in political work

Confronting sexism, racism, classism, homophobia....

Procrastination

Figuring out long- and short-term strategies for change

Coping with demands of family/lovers, jobs, and political work

Feeling "stuck" or bored in your political work

Needing a longer-term plan for your work

Getting the help you need to take difficult steps

Finding needed resources

Finding inspiration

These are some of the common difficulties faced by many of us who work for social change. Our activism may be expressed in many ways: through writing, music, dance or other art forms; through paid or volunteer work in peace, justice, or environmental organizations; through teaching, social work, health promotion, or law; through investing our money ethically; or through political work. We are using a broad, inclusive definition of activism: activism is action that contributes to "tikkun olam," a Hebrew phrase meaning the healing of our world. This includes creating our vision of the world we want to live in, not only fixing things that we see are wrong.

The rest of this section on support groups is a "how-to-do-it" manual, offered to people who are dedicated to long-term social change and who are looking for ways to sustain themselves in that work, and to people who are just setting out on that path.

There is a cultural bias in our society for doing things ourselves, "rugged individualism" and competitiveness. However, there are also models of cooperation and interdependence that go back historically to Native American societies as well as to immigrant and pioneer communities. "It is true that we are created to be individually unique," writes M. Scott Peck. "Yet the reality is that we are inevitably social creatures who desperately need each other not merely for sustenance, not merely for company, but for any meaning toourliveswhatsoever."* In social change work, cooperation is both essential and empowering. Even though individual actions can make a difference, most issues are too big for a single person to change; we can each do only our own part. Alone, each of us can lift only a corner of a big carpet; together, we can lift and move it.

This section is written as a working manual. If you are not already part of a support group, you may use its suggestions as you form one. If your group is underway this discussion of support groups may give you fresh ideas, help you prevent or solve problems that may arise, and contribute toward sustaining your group.

---

*Peck, M. Scott. "The Fallacy of Rugged Individualism." In Whitmyer, ed. *In The Company of Others*. New York: Tarcher/Perigree, 1993, p. 14.

WHY SUPPORT GROUPS?

These are not easy times for people committed to fundamental change within our society and throughout the world—for those who want to help make the world and the environment, safe, just and peaceful. For many of us this work represents a lifelong commitment. How do we sustain ourselves through the inevitable hard times? How can we hold on to our faith and resolution? Where do we recharge and renew our commitment? How do we find resources? Who can help us stay on track?

Many people have managed to continue peace and justice work without a structured support group. However, few people who devote their lives to such work do it without some regular source of reflection, challenge, and affirmation—necessary ingredients for sustained and effective efforts for change. Too often we are confronted with feelings of isolation—even from those with whom we work closely.

"The group helps me focus myself and turn to a more self-reflective state once a month about my social/political concerns," says one member of a support group. Another says "it is a safe place for me to have feelings about what is happening in the world, and the opportunity to feel and heal helps. When I do that I feel better and can keep working for the world." A third member added "I get other perspectives that I haven't thought about."

Support groups are one way to give regular attention to each person's social change work—to reflect on directions, goals, effectiveness, rough places and growing points, to challenge each other—taking into account all dimensions of our lives.

Support groups are also a way to create community. Many people long for regular opportunities for honest and open talk and practical support. Many do not find enough of this in their families, among their friends, at their place of worship, or in their neighborhoods. People often search out others who are dealing with a similar life change or situation. For example, several men in Boston, when they had children, formed a fathers' support group. The Impact Project, based in the Boston area, helps people with inherited wealth form support groups. Support groups for women with cancer have been shown to increase the life span of participants.

How Are Support Groups Different from Other Types of Groups?

In the past twenty years there has been a proliferation of groups for many purposes. For instance, women's consciousness-raising groups have proven useful for helping women understand how society is structured, and that they are not alone in feeling inadequate or angry. The success of small groups for other purposes has led us to see how they might be helpful to social change workers. But how are social change support groups different from consciousness-raising groups, therapy groups, and affinity groups?

Consciousness-raising groups assist a better understanding of elements of the world we live in—and how certain groups (for example, women and men) interact. While such groups develop a personal sense of social relationships and the dynamics of oppression, they are not necessarily organized to support the actions of individuals for social change.

Most therapy groups, as well as support groups for recovery from addiction or abuse, are oriented towards individual change and usually deal with feelings as an individual matter, not as part of a social system that needs change. Some schools of therapy (notably feminist therapy) do promote an analysis of oppression as part of the therapeutic process, but the focus remains on the individual.

Affinity groups are most often formed among people who are planning nonviolent direct action (sometimes including civil disobedience). They provide a structure for decision making and a "home base" in which to deal with feelings of fear or other concerns that arise in a potentially dangerous situation. While they certainly have an action and social change orientation, they are rarely structured to give regular, ongoing attention to each individual's work and growth. Some groups which began in the 80's as affinity groups have become support groups, or now serve both purposes.

What Is Support?

Someone once said that "support is standing so close behind your friends that the only way they can move is forward."

Support is saying "Jorge, you are on the right track, you are thinking well about your work. Keep it up!"

Support is saying "Nancy, have you thought about this aspect of the question? Try looking at it this way."

Support is saying "Jim, it looks to me as though you have lost track of your basic goals for this work. I also sense that you are on the edge of burnout, pushing yourself too hard."

One common myth about support is that it only means giving unquestioning affirmation. However, effective support is often in the form of a loving challenge based on seeing a person and their life clearly and then thinking carefully about that person. This kind of thinking is more helpful than either cheers or criticism. Most of us have to relearn how to give and receive support effectively, since it is not taught to us.

We like to imagine a time when giving and receiving this kind of loving attention to each other will be a natural part of our lives, something for which we do not need a special time and place. But, for the moment, we have found that we do need to give regular and somewhat structured form to learning and practicing the caring art of support.

The Connection between Personal and World Concerns

As we engage in social change work, personal growth, including the pain, is an important part of that work, and is intimately intertwined with it. As many have discovered, caring about the larger picture expands the context in which personal growth takes place. Issues which you thought were your own personal craziness become another signpost on the road to social change. "Through our own pain for the world we can open to power, and this power is not just our own, it belongs to others as well. It is related to the very evolution of our species. It is part of a general awakening or shift toward a new level of social consciousness."*

Fran Peavey's story illustrates this. When she heard of the mass rapes of women in the former Yugoslavia, Fran felt great sadness and concern. She felt compelled to do something for the women, meditated for many days about what to do, and came upon what she thought was a simple idea: asking her friends to make small packets of a few simple items which would communicate connection and support for women in the former Yugoslavia. She wasn't sure it was a good idea and checked it out with a few friends, and then with two women from the former Yugoslavia who were in the United States on a speaking tour. They said "what a lovely idea." Fran sent letters to about seventy friends asking them to make and send her bundles, which she planned to deliver to the women in the former Yugoslavia. When she received thousands of packages in response, she knew she had touched an anguish that many others were feeling.

---

*Macy, Joanna. *Despair and Personal Power in the Nuclear Age.* Philadelphia: New Society Publishers, 1983, p. 34.

What is an Activist Support Group?

An activist support group is a small group of people who meet regularly to give and receive reflections on each other's lives and work. This discussion of support groups will focus on groups that assist people to work more effectively for social change.

Sometimes we need help to deal with how issues affect us personally. At other times we need assistance with taking action. Therefore, support groups do not look at only one dimension of a person's life, but give attention to the emotional, the political, the spiritual, and the material. Most support groups focus on one or more of three basic elements: emotional support, support for action, and educational support.

Emotional Support

The kind of emotional support involved here is not therapy, although it may include some therapeutic methods of listening and drawing out feelings. The group may focus particularly on feelings and difficulties that get in the way of effective social change work, or feelings which arise as a natural part of such work, such as fear, anger, frustration, or joy. Emotional issues regarding personal relationships, family life, or jobs are dealt with as they affect a person's social change work. Of course, personal lives have a strong impact on social change work and cannot and should not be separated from it. For the activist support group, however, the emphasis is on work for change.

> Ellen came to her support group with a problem she had experienced in her work with a local nuclear disarmament group. She felt that others in the group did not appreciate the skills and experience she was offering. Her support group was able to see that a similar pattern was going on in her family. Ellen had recently expressed ambivalence about a trip to see her brothers and sisters whom she had not seen for over a year. As the oldest of seven and with her parents dead, she had slipped into a role of "taking care" of her siblings, so she felt unappreciated in that arena also. The support group helped her figure out how she could be with her family without taking so much responsibility for them. After the support group meeting, she had a more relaxed trip home. Later, she was able to participate more effectively in the disarmament group because she could see her tendency to take on too much and not trust that others in the group would do their work.

Support for Action

A support group can help a person clarify goals, set directions, and take action. It can also help solve problems in specific difficult situations. It encourages people to look at longer-range strategy questions. It can focus on areas of skill and leadership development for each individual. The group might also decide to undertake action projects together.

> *Nancy had recently started working with a Central America action group. They were in the process of planning for a major direct action, including the possibility of large numbers of people committing civil disobedience. The police in the city had a reputation for treating people very roughly. Nancy was concerned that the action group was not providing any training or preparation activities for people planning to take part in the civil disobedience. She had been a nonviolent action trainer years before, but felt rusty and shaky about putting herself forward to initiate training workshops for the action. Her support group helped her identify other trainers with whom she could work. They also helped her devise a strategy for gaining approval in the Central America action group for the training program.*

Educational Support

Some support groups encourage learning as a primary focus. The group might attend workshops or seminars together, read and discuss a book or books together, or ask members of the group to share special knowledge or expertise. Many people have come out of the educational system with little sense of personal power regarding learning. Support for gaining information and understanding of an increasingly complex and technically dominated world can be a crucial element of support group life.

> *The members of the all-white "Bridge" support group were interested in learning more about racism and about people of color. They started by each reading a novel or book by a person of another race, coming to support group meetings ready to share their new insights. Occasionally they all read the same book and discussed it. Once or twice they went to cultural events by African American artists. Later, they began to think together about strategies for working on white racism and then took steps to put these strategies into action.*

> *During the Gulf War a group formed whose primary goal was to share information about the war beyond what was available in the popular press and television news. The group met every weekday afternoon from five to six. People brought clippings from alternative magazines, letters from friends and family in other countries. Some people began writing about their thoughts and feelings about the war and read them aloud. The group began to compile an anthology of writing and graphic art about the war, which they intended to publish. When the war ended, they couldn't*

find a publisher and let go of that project. The group continued to meet for a while to share perspectives and then disbanded.

What Is the Role of Support Group Members?

Support group members do not have to be experts. That is, they don't have to act as therapists or as organizational consultants. Some things they do need to do are:

Listen with close attention

Ask questions (see "Strategic Questioning" later in this book)

Appreciate

Challenge

Suggest

Identify resources

Support group members do *not* need to:

Give advice when it's not asked for

Think they can solve everything

Overextend themselves

Remain quiet when they think someone is going in the wrong direction.

Over time, support group members learn how to balance appreciation and encouragement with clear and clean challenging. The most important skill is listening and encouraging people to think for themselves, supporting the self-directed process of growth, learning, and change in which we are each engaged.

At times support group members may want to give concrete support to a member who needs it. In The Gang, several members helped Amy when she moved after separating from her husband. When Bev was diagnosed with Hodgkin's disease group members took turns transporting her to the hospital for treatments. The group helped with Carol's wedding, parking cars and organizing the shared meal.

Accountability is another special element of a support group that is not always available elsewhere (especially for those of us who do social change work as volunteers). The support group is in a good position not only to encourage and challenge, but also to keep checking back on the goals people set in the group. The support group takes the goals and the individual seriously.

A support group lasts at least for a few months, and some continue for many years, allowing group members to get to know each other well and to be engaged in one another's lives as they change.

Unlike most other settings, a support group can combine and connect our spiritual, psychological and political selves in the combination or emphasis that is exactly right for the members of the group.

HOW TO START AN ACTIVIST SUPPORT GROUP

So you want to start a support group. What do you do? This chapter will take you through the steps, from inviting potential members to a sample agenda for the first meeting.

Thinking About Members

The first step in forming a support group is to decide whom you want in it. This is an opportunity to build on old friendships or turn some acquaintances into allies. Consider the following:

When looking for people you would like in your group, be sure that they share your political perspectives and activism; that you like them; and that you respect their thinking.

Think about the balance of diversity and heterogeneity you want.

> *Irene was clear at the start that she wanted a women's support group.*
>
> *Juanita wanted a Latina lesbian group; she knew a few women who were working in different organizations where they felt isolated as Latinas and thought such a group would give each of them strength.*
>
> *John, an African American, wanted a support group of environmental activists of different races, men and women; he asked Anna, a white woman, to join him and think of others to invite.*

Go after what you want. The best way to guarantee a support group you feel good about is to take initiative to form it. Consider what gifts of perspective or experience each potential member could bring.

19

Form a group with some element that holds it together: a shared interest, common values, similar experiences, the same political outlook, even a common experience of oppression (such as racism or sexism). Once the group gets going, this may become less important, but at first there needs to be some explicit bond among people. We know of men's groups, women's groups, parents' groups, groups for people with inherited wealth, teachers, anti-nuclear activists.

> *Nicholas and Eric formed a group of new fathers who were to be the primary or half-time caretakers of their infant children.*

Choose people who you judge will be able to think clearly about the others in the group, and will be insightful about the struggles of each person. Over the long haul, each person must be able to pull their weight as a thinker/listener, even though we all have periods of difficulty. One way to ensure this is to look for "peerness"—the sense of relative equality among you (this has little to do with age). Groups with very unequal skills or experience may not always work well.

Look for people with the same basic goals, expectations, or needs for the group, including expectations about how frequently and for how long the group will meet. Check these at the start and periodically throughout the group's life. If goals and expectations get out of kilter, the group will not survive long.

Don't get discouraged if the first few people say no. Use that experience to sharpen your thinking, even if you feel rejected.

Don't try to persuade someone who is reluctant or ambivalent. Listen to their reservations and give them time to think about it. If someone says yes, but they really mean no, they won't be able to bring themselves fully to the group.

Getting the Group Started

Now that you have thought about who might be in your group, you are ready to get started. Start by identifying one person you know you would like to invite. If the first person you ask isn't interested, think of another person. This may require patience; you may have a few false starts. Keep asking until there are two of you excited about forming a group. Then you can think together about a few other people to invite and find a meeting time and place.

Groups have succeeded with as few as three or four people. Some groups are as large as ten to fifteen. We find that three to ten people is best.

> *When Christopher and Anne formed their current support group, they invited another couple and three others because, given how busy they all were, it allowed one or two people to miss a meeting while the rest of the group could meet and retain its sense of being a group.*

When Irene decided, after an Interhelp workshop in 1988, that she wanted a women's support group, she approached Joan, who was also in the workshop. The two of them had read the first edition of the manual which grew into this section of the book. They made a list of women they liked, several of whom had also participated in the workshop. They invited more than the six women who came to the first meeting. At that first meeting they did a "go-around" about what they wanted to get out of the group. (In a go-around each person has a chance to speak without interruption. Often this is timed so that each participant gets equal time.) They typed this list, which they occasionally refer back to. They found one another's goals compatible, could all meet on Tuesday nights, and liked the size of the group. They decided to close membership. At the time of this writing, five years later, the group continues to meet.

The ease with which all these group members agreed on their goals and needs is unusual. It is more common to have differences about goals, difficulty about finding a time that works for everyone, or disagreement about how often people want to meet.

The First Meeting

The first meeting of a group is important because it influences people's expectations about what is possible in the group. We suggest the following goals for the first session of a support group:

Get to know one another better.

Clarify the purpose of the group.

Share each person's goals and expectations for the group.

Agree to a process that will meet people's needs.

Some groups find the following agenda outline useful for a first meeting. Your group may prefer to be more free-flowing. In any case, leave enough time; it is important not to feel rushed. Meet in a comfortable place. If it is someone's home, prepare roommates or family members so there will be as few interruptions as possible. You may want to open and/or close with a song, a moment of silence, or a short ritual, depending on what group members are comfortable doing, to develop the sense of connection in the group and to create a special tone.

Suggested Agenda for the First Meeting

Introductions

About two minutes each.

Tell how you know each other, where you live and the work you do, your involvement in social change.

Agenda Review and Recording

About five minutes.

Those who planned the meeting explain the plan. Write the agenda on a large sheet of paper or hand around copies so that everyone can see what's planned and more easily give input to the process. Planners may have to modify the original agenda. Get agreement on the agenda.

You may want to keep notes of decisions reached, an address list, and resources the group is sharing such as books, articles or videos.

Why an Activist Support Group?

About ten minutes each.

What would you like from the group? Have you been in a similar group before? What is hard for you lately in your social change work, that you might want to discuss with the group in future sessions?

Brainstorm

Five to ten minutes.

While one person writes on a big sheet of paper, other people say their fantasies or ideas or wishes for what the group might do together. Be a little wild—this is just to get ideas going, not to make a plan. You do not need to agree. (In brainstorming, the object is to generate as many ideas as possible in a stated period. To avoid the usual censoring or judging that interrupts creative thinking, the rule is that no one comments on ideas offered during the brainstorm. You can evaluate the ideas later.)

Making and Recording Agreements

Discuss for fifteen to thirty minutes.

Decide together:

> *What* the group wants to do together—choose the mix of emotional, educational and action support, based on the sharing and brainstorm above.
>
> How *often* to meet (anything from once a week to once a month is common).
>
> *How long* for each session (One and a half to four hours is common. Sharing food can be integral or added.).
>
> *Where* to meet. In some groups members take turns offering their homes to share the burdens of transport and hosting. Others prefer always to meet in the same place.

Communication Agreements

For examples, see Appendix I.

Making Commitments

About twenty to forty minutes for discussion.

Set a trial period after which the group can evaluate and people can leave gracefully if they choose to. For example, the group might decide to meet every other Wednesday from 7:00–10:00 P.M., for five meetings, and then have an evaluation session.

One person (or more) may realize in this first discussion that this group is not right for them, for any one of a number of reasons. For instance, Monica wanted a study group, not a place to share feelings. John wanted to meet weekly and everyone else wanted to meet monthly. There is someone in the group who annoys Jan terribly. Every person should feel free to say no. It is important to start out with a sense of excitement and common goals. As people agree to a trial period, ask them to make a commitment to stick with it, and to take responsibility for speaking up for their own needs.

Logistics

Ten minutes.

Choose a place, time, and someone to plan and facilitate the next meeting. Many groups find that meeting consistently on the same day of the week and time can cut short these calendar discussions. Exchange names and phone numbers.

Evaluation

About ten minutes—leave ample time.

How did this session go for people? What did people enjoy? What could be better for next time? Be sure to incorporate these suggestions into the next meeting so that people's ideas are validated.

Closing

Optional, five minutes.

Song, silence, group hug.

Suggested Agenda for a Second Meeting

Opening

Optional, five minutes.

Check-In

About ten minutes.

Decide whether you want each person to have the same amount of time or be more free-flowing. Each person tells a highlight of the week(s) since the last meeting, and/or something about their day and how they are feeling now.

Agenda Review

Ten minutes.

The person who planned the meeting has done some thinking ahead of time about issues for the group to address. He or she presents a suggested agenda to the group, asks for additions or changes, incorporates them into the agenda, and gets agreement from the group to proceed.

Life Stories

About an hour.

Members of the group take about ten minutes each to talk about significant events in their lives, including family background, when they first began to be aware of and to care about social or environmental issues, and one or two successes and difficulties in their work. Telling life stories is a good way to get to know one another, begin to recognize both common experiences and differences, and build understanding and trust.

Setting Priorities

Twenty minutes.

Working with the list generated at the first meeting about what the group might do together, the group chooses a focus or a format for the next several meetings.

For example, the group might decide to focus on learning about an issue such as urban toxic waste, or the global refugee situation, for the next several meetings, to spend half an hour each time sharing information from reading or other sources, and then to give each person time to express feelings about the issue.

Or, the group might choose to divide the time equally among members for the next few meetings in order to help each person set goals for their social change work for the next six months. You may also want to continue to include exercises designed to enable group members to know one another better or to work more effectively as a group. Several books in the bibliography of this book provide ideas.

Next Meeting

Five minutes.

Choose a time, place, and facilitator.

Evaluation

Ten minutes.

What was most useful about the meeting? Least useful? What would they change and how?

Closing

Optional, five minutes.

SUPPORT GROUP TIME: STRUCTURE AND CONTENT

We have already discussed the purpose of support groups and given some suggestions about how to start them. This chapter will offer some ideas about the structure and content of support group meetings.

Basic Ingredients of Support Group Meetings

Most support groups we know of include several basic ingredients in their meetings: an opening; an initial go-around or "check-in;" agenda review; time for group business (time and place of next meeting, facilitators, announcements); time focused on individuals in the group; time for group discussion of an issue or topic or group actions; and finally, an evaluation and closing.

An example of a group's check-in is provided in the following chapter on "Checking-In." Suggestions for managing group business are in the "What Makes Groups work" chapter. In this chapter we discuss the use of individual time in groups and ways to use study time.

Making the Best Use of Individual Time

Throughout the rest of this chapter we will refer to "individual time" or "focus time." Both of these terms refer to time set aside in the meeting to give attention to the life and work of one group member.

We've all heard that "what you get out is what you put in." We find that the focused time and attention available through support groups is rare and precious. It is most effective if careful thought is given to how to use the time well.

Irene's group decided that each person would receive about twenty minutes of individual time each meeting. Each person's time was her own. To increase safety, there would be no feedback

25

unless the person asked for it. Someone could ask to be touched, to talk, to cry and be held, to have help with a concrete task such as writing a letter. Before she left for an extended stay in Nicaragua, Barbara asked the group to do a roleplay with her about telling her parents.

Choose a Topic

In preparing for a support group meeting, think about what issue or problem will fit the time you can expect at the next support group meeting. Choose an area of your life and work that is of real concern to you at the moment. In our experience, if you can focus on a specific question, rather than a broad or vague topic, the time will be more satisfying. For instance, you might choose to focus on how you exercise leadership in a particular direct action campaign, rather than on your broader leadership questions. If the support group feels there are broader questions that should be addressed, they will bring them up!

Decide What You Want from the Group

Once you have picked a topic, figure out what you want from the group (ideas, feedback, suggestions, problem solving, appreciation, attention to feelings). For instance, you might say to the group, "I want to take the first ten minutes to describe the juicy conflict in our campaign group, then I want to hear your ideas and suggestions for the remainder of the hour."

Presentation

Think for at least a few minutes about how to present the issue, so that precious time is not wasted figuring out what to say. If you have a lot of information to present, write it up ahead of time and provide copies, or write it on large sheets of paper with felt tip pens.

How One Group Did It

At one meeting of a support group Jorge asked the group to help him devise a strategy for getting a satisfying job with political content. He presented his long-term goals for political work and the specific aspects of a job that he wished for. The group gave him feedback on his strengths and growth areas and helped him set realistic goals for a job.

Nancy was dealing with a difficult situation in her work. She started her time by saying, "I want five minutes to scream, then ten minutes to think out loud, and then fifteen minutes for the group to give me ideas and suggestions."

Jim asked the group to think with him about his tendency to isolate himself in groups where he is taking visible leadership. The group listened to him describe what has happened, then helped identify the feelings and behavior that were consistently getting in the way. Finally, they worked with him to figure out a new approach and how he could get support for trying it.

Peter used the group to help him work out a strategy for building a coalition among groups working on South Africa and on Central America. He shared some of his fears about reaching out to new people who are different from him. The group made suggestions for first steps and made a commitment to check back with Peter at later meetings to see how the work was coming.

How the Group Might Respond

Nancy finishes her brief presentation of her situation saying, "...so, there's a brief outline of my dilemma with the Task Force and upcoming meeting with the City Manager. Now I want your reactions and suggestions." The group might respond in the following ways:

Empathy and Affirmation

"Nancy, that sounds like a real tough situation! No, you're not crazy. I think anyone would be having a hard time. Your observations about the chairperson seem perceptive and sensible. Understanding people is a strength of yours..."

Help Thinking Through Options

"Nancy, you listed three possible action strategies, but I really see a fourth. Would you like to hear it?"

Observations on Personal Style or Patterns

"Nancy, it occurs to me that this is the third situation you've described where you lost your temper with a Task Force member. It seems this anger really gets in the way of your political work. Do you want to talk about that?"

The Content of Individual Time

Individual or focus time in a support group is at the crossroads of the personal and the political. We have suggested throughout this manual that support groups are devoted to each person's struggle to be effective in their political work. In this context, personal issues are particularly important as they further or hinder political work. Individuals can use their time in the group for many purposes, including:

Solve problems that arise in social change work.

Set long-term goals as a social change agent.

Identify personal difficulties that get in the way of the most effective work possible. What would it take for you to act powerfully all the time?

Assess skills and knowledge and set learning goals.

Evaluate leadership abilities—strengths and weaknesses. Set goals for leadership development.

Explore issues that are key problems for many people, such as money, families, particular oppressions (for example, as experienced by women, people of color, gays and lesbians, working class people, people with disabilities).

Receive attention nonverbally; be held, given a head or shoulder rub, or sung to.

A Meeting Format Smorgasbord

Outlined below are several different formats for support group meetings. They are quite varied in their flavor, timing and style. Pick and choose among them, invent your own, take elements of several and try a new format. It's your group. The first six formats are most relevant to emotional support or problem solving; the next two focus on study and discussion, and the last two could be appropriate for either purpose.

Equal Time

Using this format, a group gets together and quickly checks on how each person is feeling to help people bring their attention to the group and away from other things. They then divide the remainder of the time for the meeting equally among the group members.

Shorts and Longs

This group finds that they like to give a couple of people longer time each meeting and shorter time to the rest, so that they can go deeper with the "long time" people. At a typical meeting Jorge and Nancy get forty-five minutes of "focus time" (attention on them) each, while Jim and Peter get twenty minutes each on a more limited topic. At the next meeting the time allocations are switched so that Jim and Peter get "long time" while Jorge and Nancy get "short time."

A Focus on One

In this format almost all of the focus time of each meeting is devoted to one individual. This allows the group to look at a variety of factors in that person's life and explore issues deeply. Each of the other group members does a brief update with particular attention to any agreements, homework, or commitments made at previous meetings.

On the Spot

This group uses no preset agenda or time structure, but responds to the needs of the group members at the time they meet. They start with a quick check on how people are doing and what their concerns or needs are from the group. They then work together to build an agenda that will get most of the needs met. [Note: while this format may work for some groups, there is a danger that those who are more articulate about their needs or who have deeper "problems" will get more of the group's attention. If you use this format, be aware of the balance of who gets group attention over time].

In a variation of this format the facilitator checks with group members a few days before the meeting to see what they want on the agenda. That way the topics are fresh, less group time is spent on allocating agenda time, and there is a "reminder"/check-in between meetings.

The Clinic

We have heard of a group which uses a variation of "Shorts and Longs" above. The group formed around a common work interest. They spend time in each meeting doing a "clinic" on one or two specific problems that group members have encountered. One person lays out the problem and the others offer suggestions, first brainstorming alternative ways to handle the problem, then discussing them. If appropriate, the group might then do roleplays to try out some of the suggestions.

For example, a support group of trainers focused on the considerations when training people of a different race, ethnic, or class background from the trainer. First the group brainstormed all the possible "wrong moves," and then went on to generate appropriate strategies and/or attitudes. Finally, they did a series of roleplays with members of the group taking on the roles of trainer and training group participants.

A variation on this, called "Consultation," is useful because it avoids unhelpful advice giving and wanting to "fix" others' problems for them. The group asks questions (*only* questions) of the focus person to help her or him clarify how she or he wants to tackle the problem.

Large Groups: Divide and Prosper

We have heard of support groups with as many as fifteen people (although most successful groups we know of have three to ten). Since some attention to individuals is a crucial element of the support group, most of the larger groups spend at least part of their meeting time in smaller groups of three to five (or even in pairs).

Topic Time

Another common format for support groups is to choose a topic of common interest to all group members, an issue that each confronts in their work, and devote the meeting to a discussion of it. The group usually provides time for each person to reflect on their own personal experience and/or visions (models) on the subject. Common topics: leadership, class dynamics, sexism or other "–isms," conflict resolution, strategy in social change efforts.

Learners Unlimited

In recent years, many groups have been forming primarily for study and discussion. Some have been promoted by journals such as the *Utne Reader*, others by organizations such as Study Circles, others by adult education or religious organizations. Study Circles has a manual for those interested in starting study groups, and has developed curriculum guides with readings and questions for some topics. *Utne Reader* salons often focus on articles from the journal to spark their discussions.

Some groups may opt for longer sessions, or may decide to have occasional retreats.

> *In their first year of meeting, Irene's group decided to go away for a retreat, to tell one another their life stories. They enjoyed it so much, they decided to spend a weekend together in a country place once a year. Later, when Amy moved to California she returned East for the group's retreats.*

A Day in the Life

A full luxuriant day of thinking and challenging is this group's style. They get together less often, but set aside a whole day. Their format involves a series of steps as follows: a) each person quickly explains the basic issue she or he wants to deal with, then b) the other members give initial quick "brainstormed" feedback in the form of concerns, questions, or considerations on the issue, c) everyone takes time to reflect alone—using the list of concerns from the group, d) the group gets back together, divides the time equally and goes as deep as time allows on each person's issue.

The Two Day Spiritual Journey

One group gets together every three months and takes two days to worship together, meditate, search for guidance, and take time to look at each group member's journey as a spiritual and political person. The members of the group live at some distance from each other, but all have similar jobs within religious institutions. They find a lot of common themes to discuss.

CHECKING-IN

Perhaps the best way to explain a go-around, or check-in, is by example. This check-in, written up by Fran Peavey, shows how a group that has been meeting for a while functions, and gives some of its history.

Usually we meet monthly for three hours but today we decided that we wanted to take a whole day to talk about our individual cultures, and how to organize with cultural sensitivity. We met at one member's home. As the nine members entered the house, carrying their contributions for an ethnic pot luck lunch (each member brought a dish from her cultural background) one could already feel the interweaving of these lives and the work and love they share. Within ten minutes of the announced time for the meeting to start we casually find our way to our chairs. Each person has five minutes to check in.

We begin with a report that Nonnie will not be with us this month. She is in Idaho but has called several members of the group the night before. They tell how she is doing, how things have collapsed in her love life and she is needing to cool out. She has decided to take a few days to rest. Group members encouraged her to take care of herself although we will miss her. Nonnie is one of the "younger contingent" and one of the newer members of the group. She is interested in engaged Buddhism and is in the midst of a work transition.

Bev begins. She is a sixty-year-old first generation Armenian American woman who works as a substitute teacher for learning disabled students. She's doing fine in her life. Some years ago when she was diagnosed with Hodgkin's disease the group took turns transporting her to the hospital for treatments, helping her in any other way necessary. Rita was instrumental in facilitating a meeting of support group members and other people close to Bev where they talked about what would be needed and useful to help Bev through that time. Fran initially went to the doctor's office; Carol helped Bev apply for MediCal; several members gave her peer counseling sessions. She has fully recovered

31

now. She reports that lately she has been working on her photography book of nude women's bodies in unusual circumstances (e.g., over forty, pregnant). She is thrilled that a whole group of women over seventy who play Scrabble together have agreed to pose for the book. She also reports that her son was home from Russia for a few weeks. He is a photographer for Reuters and was carrying a lot of stress from the recent uprising there. Bev reports on his analysis of the part of history he is seeing. Her love for him is evident. The facilitator tells her that her five minutes is over now and our attention moves on.

Tova is a fifty-three-year-old second generation Jewish-American woman. She is feeling fine but has been very tired since returning from her trip to the former Yugoslavia where she was working with refugee women, many of whom had been raped and physically tortured. She wonders where her feelings are about what she saw. Somehow she thinks that if she could open to those feelings about the trip, perhaps her energy would return. Tova shares a little about her trip and what it has been like to come back to the U.S. She asks if people can help on Sunday when she and Fran will be giving their first public report back.

Teri, a thirty-four-year-old woman of Germanic and mixed European ancestry, is a new mother. She begins by talking about the trouble she and her husband are having getting their seventeen-month-old baby to sleep. She works for Oxfam and in a week is organizing a big event called the Hunger Banquet. She has already asked Bev to photograph the event. Berne has offered to help with tasks and Teri hopes others will come and help. Does anyone know someone who could videotape the event for a publicity video Oxfam is thinking about? Several people give suggestions which will be followed up in the break. Teri reports also that she and her family are going to Ecuador on a combination family vacation and research trip for Oxfam. She is concerned about traveling with such a young child. Bev nods in shared knowledge of the troubles of traveling with children and they agree to share ideas at the break of ways to make the traveling easier on all concerned.

Rita is next. She was raised Catholic and is originally from Chicago although she has been in the Bay Area for many years. Rita is forty-five years old and makes her living as a nurse in a psychiatric ward of a hospital. Rita is one of the old-timers, having been in the group twelve years. When Rita had hepatitis the group took on major responsibility for getting her food and organizing a list of her friends to bring it in. She reports on her trip home, on some of the issues in her large family. She is particularly concerned about one of her nieces who is having troubles. Her job is more intense these days because of a scare around AIDS in her hospital. Her organizing in her neighborhood is going well but one woman has taken over the group and does not let others share in the power. We all agree to think with her about this issue later.

Berne is back in the group for a few months, after living in Budapest for a year. Berne is fifty years old, Jewish, trained in community organizational development. Just now she has completed the first draft of a book about Hungary and freedom and has been offered another book contract. She is exhilarated about the feedback her editor is giving her. She will be working at her old job as a community organizer in a food program. Berne shares with us how things are going with her daughter who has just gone to Italy to work as a nanny and is not happy in this job. Teri suggests a book with opportunities for young people overseas. [We actually have agreed not to talk during check-ins but we fall out of this agreement regularly, and, in fact, as long as we don't get into advice-giving and long discussions, we feel comfortable with flexibility about this agreement.]

It's Carol R.'s turn. She is a mother of two young boys, and is proud of her Jewish ancestry. She reports that her husband has a new job. There are some good things about this and some new strains in the family. He is not entirely happy with the pressure in the new job and he has to wear a suit every day. Carol's own job as a social worker is undergoing some special stresses this week, as someone from the Clinton administration is coming to investigate the approach her office has to preserving families. Carol will be one of the people giving information to the researcher and she is excited about being in this position. She must leave the group midday as she is being cut short in her time with her children by this researcher coming on Monday, so will make up the time in the afternoon today. Everyone supports her values with her children and talks for a bit about how to arrange the schedule of the day so Carol can participate in the parts of the agenda she is most interested in.

Gently the time-keeper reminds us all that it is time to move on.

Amy is next. Amy is thirty-three years old, a Chinese-American who makes her living as a technical writer. Amy announces she has received a salary raise at work (everyone congratulates her and makes gestures of approval with their hands). She is moving to a place where she can live alone. She explains that she has never lived alone and is really looking forward to it. Several people helped her move last time and they are confused why she is moving so soon. Amy talks more about the move. She went back east to a gathering of her old support group in Boston last week. One of the members of that group was asking for special support as she goes through a particularly difficult time in her life and Amy wanted to be there for her.

It's Carole's turn. She is Jewish, in her early fifties. She works as a fundraiser for a small progressive nonprofit organization. She reports about a conflict at work and how it is affecting her life. Her mother and father are aging. She has a new darling grandchild, so thinking about the generations is on her mind.

I was the last one to check in and for the life of me I cannot remember what I said. But I am fifty-two years old, of mixed mostly European and a little Native American heritage.

The meeting moved into agenda review and we were off. It was a great day.

WHAT MAKES
GROUPS WORK?

In order to be effective, groups need clear goals and structure, an atmosphere of trust, good listening skills, and full participation. This chapter outlines some key elements of group process.

Establishing Clear Agreements

It's important that group members agree about such issues as how frequently and where to meet, how to deal with lateness and absences, whether and when to add members, and what the content of meetings will be.

Take time to discuss differences and make decisions about these issues; you will learn more about one another's wishes, needs and boundaries. This process also helps to clarify what you expect of one another and to practice negotiation.

> *Although the Earthworms had made an agreement to start meetings at 7:00 sharp, several members were consistently late. The others waited for them, feeling resentful. Finally Cathy put the issue of time on the agenda. Peter and Mary said they often got stuck in rush hour traffic and asked to change the starting time to 7:30. The group agreed to the change and also agreed that all those present at the starting time would begin without waiting for latecomers.*

Group Decision Making

There are many ways of reaching decisions in groups. Peace and social justice groups often make decisions by consensus, a process through which the whole group seeks a decision to which all members can agree. Some groups vote and decide by majority rule. Other groups decide by consensus but have a fallback of voting if a decision is not reached within a reasonable length of time.

One visual way of finding out whether there is consensus is the "thumbs" method. When someone has a clear proposal, the facilitator asks for a show of thumbs up if members agree, thumbs down if they disagree, and thumbs sideways if there are questions. If all the thumbs are up, the proposal has consensus. If not, discussion is needed. Usually a modified version of the original proposal emerges that takes into account the needs and concerns of everyone in the group. On important issues and for principled reasons, it is possible for one person to block consensus. That person may have valuable concerns that others have overlooked.

Although this method usually takes longer than a majority vote, it does assure that people hear one another's ideas and feelings. If a quick vote yields a decision that a number of people are unhappy with, the resulting difficulties may be more time consuming and stressful to resolve than working out a decision by consensus. If you are unfamiliar with different kinds of decision making, there are a variety of books listed in the bibliography. Take time in your group to choose which method or methods you want to use.

Creating an Atmosphere of Trust

Trust grows in a group as people get to know one another more deeply, learn to deal with differences and resolve conflicts, and respect decisions that the group has made. In early meetings, leave time for people to tell their stories in some kind of structured way (for example, group members might each take ten minutes to tell their histories as activists, or to talk about what makes them afraid, or a time when they felt powerful).

In every meeting, it helps to take time at the beginning to "check in," to say something about how each person is feeling that day. This can bring valuable awareness about what is going on in people's lives, and enable members to be more present for the rest of the meeting. [This practice can be used at the beginning of business meetings, such as committees, task forces or board meetings, as well as in support groups.]

Trust may be eroded unless group members feel assured that personal things they say will not be repeated outside the group. Such an agreement to "confidentiality" is important to establish early in the life of the group.

Confidentiality is one of a number of communication agreements your group might consider. You may want to brainstorm a list and write them down to keep and refer to. Two examples can be found in Appendix I: Group Process Resources. One was written for communities by Carolyn R. Shaffer and Kristin Anundsen*; the other, The "Ten Commandments" for Group

---

*Schaffer, Carolyn R., and Kristin Anundsen. *Creating Community Anywhere*. New York: Tarcher/Perigree, 1993, p. 252.

Conversation, was conceived by Elissa Melamud, who developed support groups called "peace circles" in the 1980 s.

Another aspect of establishing trust is building an expectation in the group that when agreements are broken they will be dealt with, and that, when disagreements or conflicts arise they will be addressed. This is not easy; most of us have difficulty welcoming or embracing conflict and we tend to avoid it. The next chapter provides some suggestions about dealing with broken agreements and conflict resolution.

Group Participation Skills

Even when a group has a designated facilitator, the more every participant assumes some responsibility for moving the group forward, the more satisfying and effective meetings will be. Here are some skills that enhance the process of support groups:

Speak directly and personally

Say what *you* think and feel about the issues being discussed. Avoid generalizations, blaming, accusatory language, and jargon. Be specific and use examples. Use "I language," stating observations, not assumptions. An example of effective and ineffective language follows:

> *Effective:* "I feel frustrated and resentful when our meetings go past ten o'clock. I would like us to keep to our agreement to end by ten o'clock."

> *Ineffective:* "People are being really irresponsible about keeping to time. Meetings have been running over constantly and everyone gets upset, but no one does anything about it."

The way a message is conveyed to a group will have a large part in determining how the group responds.

Allow for silence

At times when discussion is profound or emotions are strong it may be helpful to build in a moment of silence. Pausing between speakers in a discussion can also cut down on interruptions and allow people to take in fully what each person contributes.

Allow for variety of expression

People have different ways of expressing their thoughts and feelings. Respect each person's style. For instance, some people require time to think before speaking. In a group where other people operate at a fast pace, a more deliberate person would begin to feel lost and unheard.

Balance appreciating and challenging one another

It's impossible to receive too much appreciation, especially in political work. Almost everyone suffers from feeling that he or she is not doing enough and is not receiving enough appreciation or rewards. Be sure each person receives specific, verbal appreciation for what they do. Each person may also need a challenge to take the next step or try something new.

Respect feelings

Talking about social change work or personal experiences can bring up anger, sadness, or other feelings. Your group may feel much less comfortable with some feelings than with others. Many people carry with them strong messages about feelings. "Men don't cry" is one example. You may want to include a communication agreement about feelings, such as "It's alright to express anger as long as no one in the group is put down or physically hurt."

Talking about current difficulties tends to bring up old feelings about family, work, and past successes and failures, including feelings which seem unrelated to the current situation. The group may take time to talk about these feelings, or help members decide how those feelings can get dealt with outside the group. We help each other become more effective activists by dealing with feelings, both past and present, while remembering that we are not being therapists. Support groups cannot replace professional help when it is needed.

Respect group members and avoid putdowns

The language we use is important. It is fine to disagree with someone, but this can be done while conveying caring and respect for the person.

> *Jorge was annoyed with Peter and said, "You silly kid, how could you think that?" Peter, the youngest member of the group, was offended. Nancy stepped in: "Jorge, you have a right to disagree with Peter. Could you say it again without putting him down?"*

Keep on track

When you think that a discussion is going off on a tangent, say so, and remind others of the topic you were discussing.

Respect time

If you have agreed about how much time your group will spend on various agenda items, each group member can take some responsibility for paying attention to time, and not leave it solely to the facilitator to keep things going.

Roles that Help a Group Function Well

We have found that a group functions well when someone is thinking systematically about what the members of the group need, what is happening in the group (interactions among members), and what steps need to be taken to move things along. This role can be shared by everyone in the group, but it is also useful to designate particular roles for specific meetings. If you rotate the roles among all group members, each person gets practice taking responsibility for the group's life and health.

Some of the roles that can be played by group members are described below. Not all roles are necessary at all meetings, but if the group is having difficulties they may become more crucial.

Facilitator

The facilitator's task is to help the group stay focused and move through the agenda, to pay attention to the beginning and ending of meetings and to transitions. The facilitator plans the agenda, either before the meeting or with the group at the beginning of the meeting; pays attention to each group member during the meeting, making sure that everyone is heard; and keeps the meeting moving. Since this is a lot for one person to do, the group may want to designate a separate person as "vibes watcher" (see below) and someone else as a time-keeper. The group may also wish to have a notetaker for parts of the meeting.

Most people can develop the skills needed to facilitate a meeting. Each group will need to decide whether facilitation will be rotated, done by the same person each time, or whether the group will function without a designated facilitator.

> Irene's group has been meeting for several years. The six members know one another well, and all have good communication skills. They have decided not to have a designated facilitator, but to all be aware of what needs to happen at each meeting.

> The Gang has two co-facilitators each meeting. Everyone takes a turn. Newer members grow in confidence when they co-facilitate with longer-term members. By working together, the co-facilitators get to know one another better, balance one another's strengths, and share the responsibility.

"Vibes Watcher"

The job of the "vibes watcher" is to notice what is going on, decide whether to bring it to the group's attention, describe to the group what is happening, ask what they want to do about it, or give attention to specific people.

> When Jim was "vibes watcher," he noticed that Nancy, who was facilitating the meeting, had gotten engrossed in a discussion

with Peter, and was losing her focus on the whole group. The other two members of the group looked sleepy and restless. After Jim mentioned it, the group decided to go on with the discussion, but suggested that Nancy ask someone else to facilitate for that part of the meeting.

Sarah was aware, an hour into the meeting, that everyone in her group looked sleepy. Even though it wasn't break time, she suggested a group stretch, which the others enjoyed.

Time-keeper

The time-keeper lets the group know when the time allowed for a topic is nearly over, and when the allotted time has been used up. The group can then decide to move on to the next topic, or it may choose to stay longer with the first topic. This role can help a group stay focused. When there are co-facilitators, one may watch the time while the other facilitates, or the role can be taken by a group member.

Recorder

The recorder keeps notes on important decisions. The group may want to have a notebook or folder for these notes, group photos, drawings, letters, or other memorabilia.

Taking Care of Group Business

Group business usually comes near the beginning and the end of meetings and includes the agenda review, logistics, announcements and an evaluation of the meeting.

Agenda preparation and review

If at all possible, plan the agenda before the meeting. This is usually done by the facilitator(s) with input from group members.

The week before the monthly meeting of The Gang, the two co-facilitators call members to find out whether they want focus time and to get suggestions for a topic for the whole group to explore. Based on these calls, they plan an agenda, including how much time each item will take, write it all on newsprint, and present it to the group.

Even with this kind of planning it is important to review the agenda with the group and to allow for changes. In presenting the agenda, the facilitator gives a brief idea of what is to be covered and how, explaining the rationale for the order of the agenda. If someone suggests a change, check it out with the group before changing it. As facilitator your responsibility is to the whole group.

After you have presented the agenda and made any changes, ask members if they are willing to accept it. Then you will have a shared agreement about the structure of the meeting.

Logistics

Even if group business is minimal, be sure to leave time for it. This may include setting meeting dates and places if these vary, who will facilitate if this role rotates, who will follow up on tasks that emerged in the meeting, who will call members who are absent.

Evaluation

Evaluating a meeting provides time to reflect on what happened. It enables people to leave with a sense of closure, rather than with regrets or appreciations about things that happened that may go unexpressed. Evaluation can take the form of a quick brainstorm of what people felt good about and what could have been better, or a go-around where each person comments on how the meeting went. Useful suggestions can be incorporated into future meetings.

Celebrate Your Group

In your support group don't just focus on work and difficult issues. Take time to have fun with each other and include more lighthearted activities in your regular meetings. Some suggestions:

Break Bread Together

Food is a wonderful community builder. Many support groups include meals or snack breaks in their meeting times, bringing food to share, or prepared by a few members.

Celebrate Anniversaries

Birthdays or the anniversary of the group itself are great opportunities for taking time out for more frivolous activities. Have fun!

Acknowledge Successes

The hardworking members of your support group are committed to challenging, long-term struggles for social change. Use the group to acknowledge how you are each making a difference. Many people find it difficult to appreciate their own successes, may not see the value of congratulating others' achievements, or may feel embarrassed when they are appreciated by others. Tell them why it is important to do it, and once they take part the value will usually be obvious.

Be specific. If some special event takes place (a campaign has a success, someone gets that perfect job...) celebrate. In general, we need ongoing ways to affirm the real steps forward we make, even if the journey is a very long one.

The Gang also celebrates the successes of others. Occasionally the group gives an award for service to humanity when they hear of someone who has done great work. They have printed a certificate that every member signs and they send it off.

Disbanding is Fine: Appreciate and Evaluate

Even the best of support groups will, at some point, come to an end. Group members may encounter changes in their lives. People move away. The group may also serve well for a time and then become less relevant to its members. Or the group may decide to disband because of internal conflicts that cannot be resolved.

No matter what the cause for a group's ending, there is a lot to be gained from a careful evaluation. Schedule a special meeting to wrap up. It can include time for people to reflect on what they have learned from the group, and to share some of the ways the group has been helpful to them. Look also at ways the group did not function well and why, in order to carry learning rather than bad feelings into other groups and situations. Take time to appreciate each other.

TYPICAL
DIFFICULTIES AND
HOW TO RESOLVE THEM

Groups may get off to a good start and then fall apart. Difficulties often arise in these areas: goals, broken agreements, comings and goings, differences or conflicts not dealt with, individual styles, breaches of trust, and subgroups.

Goals

Even when a group starts out with clear goals, members' lives and interests change, and local and world events may affect the group. Meetings may no longer serve the needs of participants.

> The Earthworms began as a study group focusing on urban toxic waste. Six months later, the group decided to get involved in a community garden in a vacant lot in their neighborhood. Bill brought up his concern that the group was changing its focus from a study to an action group. While group members were enthusiastic about the garden project, they wanted to continue to learn about toxic waste. They decided to meet once a month as a study group and to spend three mornings a month working in the garden. This agreement satisfied Bill and he stayed in the group.

It is also possible that this change would not have been acceptable to Bill. He might have decided to leave the group or to attend only the study group sessions.

The best remedy is to take time to clarify the purpose of the group not only at the beginning, but also any time later on when it becomes unclear or no longer meets the needs of some group members. It may be helpful to plan to do this at regular intervals, such as every six months or year.

Maintaining Agreements

Even though everyone in the group has agreed to attend regularly, to come on time, and to follow communication agreements, people may forget, grow careless, or simply interpret them differently from others. This is bound to create resentments.

Erratic attendance may be a sign of low commitment to the group. Your group may want to have as one of its shared agreements an understanding about attendance, how many meetings a member may miss, and whether someone will phone absent members.

> *Linda found herself missing meetings of her support group and forgetting to call someone in the group beforehand. When Jorge called her to ask why she wasn't there, she realized she didn't want to be part of the group and decided to leave.*

> *In the Earthworms, one member frequently broke in with comments or questions during check-ins, even though the group had agreed that that time would be uninterrupted. Nancy brought up her concern. The member apologized and began doing it less often, though he still needed occasional reminders.*

> *Brigit fumed that once again the group was starting thirty minutes late. "Oh," Josh said, "I thought that the first half hour was just an arrival, informal time." The group decided to start promptly fifteen minutes after the scheduled time.*

Comings and Goings

People may want to leave the group, or join the group once it is underway. When someone wants to leave, or does leave, take the time to deal with it. Make time for goodbyes, and talk about the person's contributions to the group. A member's leaving is a loss to the group and may bring up feelings.

> *When Liz moved to Ithaca she had to leave The Gang, which she had been part of for several years. Before she left, the group planned a meeting that focused on Liz. They gave her time to talk about her excitement and fear about the move, about the job she was going to, her concern about finding an apartment and good schools for her children. Then each member told Liz what they appreciated about her and how she had been important in the life of the group.*

When considering the addition of new members to the group, think about such things as the optimum size of your group and what qualities a new person could bring to the group that might balance those of people in the group.

Allow to surface and deal with any reservations people have. Come to consensus as a group so that you can truly welcome a new person.

> When Amy moved across the country her group decided not to take a new member. The group had built up so much trust that they thought of themselves as an extended family. Once a year they had a weekend retreat and Amy flew back to be with them whenever she could.

> In contrast, when Liz moved to Ithaca, her group added someone new. They thought about people they knew who might like to join the group, and who would bring something new to the group. When they agreed on inviting Nonnie, Rita, who knew her best, briefed her about the group's focus and history and asked her to come to a meeting. After the meeting Rita called everyone and found unanimous agreement to welcome Nonnie to the group.

It is important for the group to have a process for selecting, inviting, and integrating new members. For example, if one person has a friend they want to invite to the group, and someone else doesn't want to be in a group with that person, what will you do?

Dealing with Differences

Every group is bound to include people with some differences. Acknowledge and value those differences, whether they have to do with age, gender, sexual preference, class background, race or religion, or parental status. The more you learn about one another, including learning about one another's backgrounds, the more you will be able to appreciate and trust one another. Many of these differences have led to experiences of oppression in the past or in the present. Your group may want to read about or share your own experiences with oppression and how to recognize and deal with it in the group. Story telling is a valuable tool.

> When Sam's support group decided to spend half a day giving each person time to talk about his or her cultural background, he decided to use his time telling about coming out as a gay man. He wanted the others to know that his journey had not been easy. He also wanted them to hear what he loves about being gay. And he wanted them to honor his relationship with his partner as they did the relationships of heterosexual members of the group.

Individual Styles

One person may talk too much or ramble. Another person may have difficulty expressing feelings, and always say, "Everything is fine". Someone else may be seriously depressed. If any of these behaviors bothers you, talk about it in the group, with care and respect. It is important to distinguish between personality traits that are annoying and unlikely to change and distress in response to a current situation in someone's life. In the former case, it may be necessary to accept the person's behavior or leave the group, unless that person is breaking an agreement. An example of situational distress follows:

> *In early meetings of his support group, Jeremy noticed that Larry joked every time someone in the group expressed strong feelings, and invariably drew the attention of the group to himself. Jeremy became increasingly annoyed with Larry and decided to bring it up in the group. When he did, he found that others were also irritated, and that they were also concerned about Larry. Larry disclosed that he had recently learned that his father had cancer and needed surgery, and that his worries kept him from listening to others in the group. The group encouraged him to take time in the group to talk about his situation and to share his feelings. It was easier for Larry to listen to others after that.*

If Larry had continued to joke a lot and Jeremy had continued to be annoyed, others in the group would have needed to address this conflict.

Interpersonal Conflicts and Subgroups

When interpersonal conflicts arise in a group, it is best to acknowledge them rather than hope that they will go away with time. A group member may want to act as a mediator, especially if she or he has training or experience with conflict resolution. Such training is available from community dispute resolution centers in many cities. If the group cannot resolve the conflict using its own resources, it may wish to invite someone from outside to facilitate one or two meetings, to help the group deal with the conflict and teach some conflict resolution skills. For those who want to learn more about conflict resolution, there are many excellent books on this topic listed in the bibliography.

Subgroups may emerge when two or more members have an intense personal relationship (they may be lovers or ex-lovers, or have a long history), when several members of a group share other activities or friends, or have something else in common.

> *In one group of three, Joan and Alice were lesbians and Julia was married and heterosexual. Julia felt uncomfortable talking about her relationship with her husband, thinking that Joan and Alice wouldn't be interested or sympathetic. When Julia was able to discuss her discomfort about this issue with Joan and Alice, it enabled the three women to talk about their differences and their liking and appreciation of one another.*

If you are able to welcome conflict into your group, rather than avoid it, you may learn a lot about yourself and one another, and communicate in ways that promote understanding and creative outcomes.

SUSTAINING A
GROUP OVER TIME

There are many benefits in belonging to a support group that continues for a long time. These are described by Jane, a member of Ahimsa for about eight years, and by Berne, a member of The Gang.

Jane's Story

Ahimsa began as an affinity group organized around a specific antinuclear action in 1984. The action involved civil disobedience and vigiling. There was a high degree of commitment and involvement. Four or five women from this early group are still members of Ahimsa.

I joined in 1985. Antinuclear actions were diminishing and the focus was shifting to Central America. I had been to Nicaragua with Witness for Peace. Within the next year I helped plan a trip Ahimsa took to Honduras and El Salvador in 1986. We contacted women's groups there, and on returning presented slide shows and a show of children's art. That was our last major action as a group.

Some members are strong activists still, and some have focused elsewhere. I went into another chapter of my life where my service energy was limited to my work as a psychotherapist and I explored creative expression through dance and voice improvisation. Now I am in support groups for performers who express their activism through performing.

When I switched my focus it was a painful process for me. Although others in Ahimsa went through similar changes I was at first most vocal about it in the group. I feared that I would be judged, that I was being hedonistic. I experienced loss because I couldn't do everything. I had also been involved in the Fellowship of Reconciliation. I began to see less of those people and Central America activists. I got clear support from people in Ahimsa and no judgment, a process that I think further bonded us.

47

Now most people in Ahimsa have shifted their focus and the group is no longer a vehicle for common projects. A couple of women who wanted the group to be more project oriented dropped out. Those who stayed wanted to become closer, to know each other in a more personal way. We didn't fully talk out or make decisions around the process we were going through. We have a tremendous precedent of acceptance, which is wonderful, but I think, some typical avoidance of processing conflict areas which limits our growth or closeness.

Sometimes now individuals suggest things for the group to do which we occasionally do but more often we don't. Everyone wants to continue in the group even though they don't come every time. We have shared values, a shared world view, and a hunger for community. Most of us don't have a specific community; we have bits of community here and there. Ahimsa gives us mutual support: personal, social and spiritual. We know that the group will celebrate changes in life style. We invite each other to weddings and birthdays. We have spent quite a few years together witnessing the evolution of each other's lives. The core of who we are is stable.

Berne's Statement

This has indeed been a support group for me, through some difficult times, as well as some real highs. What I most deeply appreciate is the feeling of acceptance within the group that continues through the good times and the bad. I like that this is not a place for competitiveness or ambition. I like the feeling that we share a concern for the condition of the world, that we all feel a sense of responsibility to try to make a positive contribution, and that we can unselfconsciously use the group as a safe place to think about our personal role in the greater scheme of things. Somehow this particular collection of people manages to take these things seriously, without taking ourselves too seriously.

Changing Needs of Members

Groups that last for several years or more often need to change in structure or content to meet the changing needs of members and to keep meetings alive and interesting. They may also change to reflect changing national or international conditions. This section is a series of vignettes that may provide ideas for groups that are dealing with transitions or losing energy.

Changing personal situations

Carol was single when she joined her support group. A few years later she married Scott. The group was all there, helping with transportation coordination, directing parking in a small spot, organizing the pot luck, assisting with clean up. Later, when Carol *had children, if Scott was unable to babysit the day of the meeting, the group contributed money for Carol's child care.*

After being in his support group for a while, Jim discovered that he was HIV+. He told the group reluctantly, afraid they might distance themselves from him. Two members decided to join a group for friends and family members of those who are HIV+. Others read about HIV and AIDS. The group was able to talk with Jim about what kind of support he needed, to provide concrete help, such as going to medical appointments with him and walking his dog on days when he felt too tired, as well as providing emotional support.

The Gang recognized that several members were working independently. They decided to have a sub-support-group called the "Monday Club" which acted like a staff meeting. They met on Monday mornings, when each person set goals for the week and checked on the goals set the previous week.

Changing national or international issues

Recently the Ahimsa group decided to act together in response to Fran Peavey's request for packages for women victims of war in the former Yugoslavia. They spent a meeting making packages, taking polaroid photos of the group to include, and writing messages for the women. Although in its early life the group had participated in many actions together, their focus had changed to more personal sharing, and this action was an unusual thing for them to do.

John's support group, Desert Life, which began during the Gulf War, to meet the needs of members to talk openly with others and learn more about the war, continued to meet afterwards and to study other issues they were less informed about. They read about 500 years of European colonization of the Americas, about ecological issues, about free trade agreements and their implications.

During the Gulf War, The Gang spent one meeting sewing patches for a quilt for the women of Iraq, part of a peace gesture from women in the United States.

Changing the focus of a group

The Black Sweaters began as a civil disobedience affinity group, inspired by the women of Greenham Common in England. They participated in many actions and became part of the Pledge of Resistance. As the women got to know one another better through actions and potlucks they also began to give one another support about finding meaningful work, coming out to family members, dealing with childhood abuse.

Varying content of meetings

The Gang specializes in telling stories. Every once in a while they start a new cycle. Each person has about twenty minutes to tell a story about a certain topic. Sometimes the group asks questions, sometimes the person simply speaks. The stories may be a string of vignettes or may go deeper about one or two experiences. The themes have included spiritual stories, political stories, work stories, relationship stories, sexual stories, money stories and house stories.

The Earthworm support group decided to add outdoor experiences to their study sessions and garden mornings. They scheduled periodic hikes, and an all-day challenge ropes course at a local outdoor education center. Several members expressed greater trust in others in the group after this experience, because there were moments in the day when they literally had to trust one another with their lives.

Rituals

Irene's support group ends every meeting with one or two songs. Group members stand in a circle, link arms and sing.

The Earthworms begin meetings with five minutes of silent meditation. Then whoever is facilitating reads a poem or an earth prayer to the group.

Sarah, who is a yoga teacher, doesn't like to sit for too long. She initiated a stretch break in the middle of the Earthworms' meeting time. Different members take turns leading the stretches.

The Gang created an "appreciation day" for members where outside friends who knew of the social change work of members of the group joined them to express their appreciation.

There is no limit to ways in which groups can be together. If your group is beginning to feel stale, it may be useful to consider whether some aspect of individual or group life is being overlooked. If your group mostly talks, doing something physical or spiritual, or introducing music or art, can bring new life.

Seeding New Groups

Groups that have stayed together for a while may find that friends or colleagues ask to join the group. If the group is not taking new members, it may want to help seed a new group. Individual members may serve as consultants to help new groups get started, or the group may have an open meeting, picnic, or other event to bring together those who want to be part of a group.

Leaders of workshops dealing with a range of social change issues may also find that some participants desire to continue to meet as a support group after the workshop ends. This is most likely to succeed if people are able to meet quickly, exchange phone numbers, and pick a time for a follow-up meeting while they are still together. Alternately, a leader may invite participants to fill out a survey with their schedules and goals and the leader (or a volunteer) can organize one or more support groups to convene at a later date.

> *Rita, of The Gang, acted as a coordinator to help people find affinity groups in the eighties. She asked a series of questions to help people focus on their needs. These included how far people wanted to travel to meetings, how often they wanted to meet, whether they wanted to focus on action or education, what common attributes they felt were important. She gave people phone numbers of others whose preferences were similar, and was available to consult as groups began to form.*

SUPPORT GROUP BLESSING

May the life of your support group be a full circle.
May it be nourishing.
May its roots deepen and its leaves be green, its fruit plentiful.
May it experience all the seasons of the year
    and die with dignity when it is time.

"The Gang." Photographed by Bev Ramsay

Section II

CLEARNESS FOR INDIVIDUAL DECISION MAKING

by Peter Woodrow

INTRODUCTION
TO CLEARNESS

A Personal Story about Clearness

Late last spring I was feeling dissatisfied with my work. I had been providing organizational development consulting services to nonprofit groups and also doing occasional training in conflict resolution. It didn't seem to hang together for me and I was getting very tired of working alone most of the time, since nonprofit groups can rarely afford to hire a team. Meanwhile, I had applied for a job as director of a major institute within an academic institution, but found myself feeling profound ambivalence about that kind of institutional position. At about the same time, a large social change organization I had been associated with for many years was undergoing reorganization and several new high-level positions were being created. The executive director asked me if I was interested in applying for any of these new positions.

After stewing for some time, I decided that I should follow my own advice and call a clearness committee for myself. Within a few weeks I found a time when the members of a small clearness group could get together. The group was three people plus me: an old political ally, friend and current housemate; another old friend who had also been in a support group with me for several years; and another friend who knows me through Quaker circles and through sharing music. In preparation for the meeting, I wrote up a four page description of the various directions I was considering, including a quick analysis of the positives and negatives I felt about each choice, and a list of my various commitments. I distributed the paper to the group members before the meeting.

The process for this meeting was fairly informal. I asked that we start with silent worship and then said a few things to add to what I had already shared in the paper. I surprised myself and members of the group by expressing a need to understand and act on my "ministry" in the world, which for me had a spiritual dimension and a dimension based on where I feel excitement and energy—what we called my "heart work." I have felt drawn for many years toward conflict resolution work in the international arena; this is my heart work. As a Quaker, there has always been an implicit spiritual dimension to much of what I do, but I talked about the need to make spirituality more explicitly present in my life and work. To my surprise, as I finished my remarks about this, a couple of people in the group were in tears—here was a level of caring, pain, and joy I had not expected.

The group began to respond to the information I had given out and the things I had said. They urged me to find a way to pursue my heart work, even though it might be difficult to find a paid position in that arena. At times individuals in the group started to get into quick exchanges and debate. When this happened, we called the group back to a mode of listening with a more spiritual tone. The doubts I was feeling about taking more institutional jobs were examined and the group confirmed that those positions would cut me off from the contributions I really want to make. The group also encouraged me to look for ways to build a local diverse team of conflict resolution and organizational development folks to work with in the long term.

I left the meeting feeling rededicated to work I care about deeply, supported in my tentative choice of direction, and challenged to give regular attention to my spiritual life and growth. I also felt buoyed up by the caring and thoughtful attention of members of my community.

What Is Clearness?

In simple terms, clearness brings a small group of four to eight people together to help one person, whom we will call the "focus person," clarify a present reality or determine a future direction in regard to career, relationships, family, social change work, religious calling and so on.*

Why is a clearness process necessary or important? There was a time when many people lived, worked, worshiped, married, birthed, played, and struggled with and among one group of people—their community. Those communities knew their boundaries, knew who was in and who was out, and knew what kinds of behavior were acceptable and what were not. Individuals were engaged at every level; they knew their place and function in society. When they were confused, there were many sources of guidance, both from rules and norms and from individuals in the community (ministers, priests, elders, relatives). Such a life had wonderful aspects, providing a caring, nurturing, and supportive environment. It also felt constraining and rigid to some.

Much has been written about alienation and isolation in modern industrialized society. Many aspects of life which were once integrated into multi-dimensional communities have become compartmentalized and private.

---

*The clearness process was originally developed by Quakers, and it has been adapted for use by social change activists and other religious communities. (See the article, "A Brief History of Clearness among Quakers and Others," in Appendix II.)

Today it is possible for an individual to go to school and college, marry, raise children, work at a job for many years, retire and expire, all without significant interaction with a community that either cares or constrains. While few live such purely alienated lives, many people feel an element of that disconnection. Many seek re-engagement with a caring community, where they can find both support and accountability for their lives and actions.

Clearness stands at the intersection of individuals and their communities; it is a way to directly involve the community in important decisions by individuals. Clearness acknowledges, in part, that the decisions of individuals have an effect on the broader group—and *vice versa*. For faith communities clearness is a practical reflection of the idea that "we are all part of one another." Clearness provides a way that the personal process of spiritual discernment can be nurtured by the religious community. For social action groups, clearness reminds us that each of us is engaged in a long-term struggle towards inspiring visions and against powerful forces—which we can't do alone. Clearness helps maintain the integrity of our own witness as we face larger social forces and the demands of those dearest to us.

Clearness does not imply "clearance." The clearness group aids the focus person in seeking clarity, not permission or approval. In other words, the group engages in a process of mutual searching for the right way forward. The sense of "rightness" about a proposed action is often experienced as a new clarity, based on insights discovered during the clearness meeting. Even though this is a group endeavor, which benefits from the special chemistry of group interaction, the decision ultimately remains with the individual who brought the dilemma or problem to the group.

Clearness meetings do contain an element of judgment; the members of the group are not asked to blindly approve and support a proposed new direction or action by the focus person. Rather, the group listens closely, pools its wisdom and insights, and may, in some cases, challenge strongly. Dearly held assumptions may be tested and fail. Self-imposed expectations or expectations laid on the focus person by others may prove groundless. Creativity may emerge from unexpected places.

Clearness, at its best, is an expression of connection between individuals and their communities. It expresses the idea that we seek clarity together, collectively and individually. We are not alone in our efforts to be our truest selves and to discover our deepest integrity.

When to Use Clearness

Social change activists, religious groups, and cooperative communities have used clearness processes for a variety of purposes. Individuals who are at important choice points in their careers or personal lives have used it: in deciding to stay or move away, to pursue additional schooling or keep working, to change careers or revitalize the present one, to commit to a social justice campaign or concentrate on earning money, to leave a relationship or move towards stronger commitment, to have a child or not.

The impetus for this kind of personal search can arise from several quarters. Perhaps it is dissatisfaction with a job or feeling underappreciated in it. Maybe there is an old dream that has not been fulfilled. Political events may also present a new challenge. Some people will be presented with an alluring opportunity. Others will embark on a deliberate period of search for the right way forward. The natural changes and rhythms of our lives bring us to new perspectives and new challenges.

> There can be times in our lives when an utterly logical course, which was previously satisfying, suddenly seems barren or false—or it may just close down, forcing us into painful re-examination of the way we are to go. We may be seized by a sudden conviction that it is time to break with our past and begin some particular new venture. Sometimes we are going along contentedly enough when a new possibility that requires serious consideration is presented to us. Those who know us may begin to name a new thing in us that needs to be honored. Or we may wake one morning to find that a slow process of which we've been only marginally aware has crystallized, with a host of implications.*

In religious communities, the occasion for clearness may arise in a different way, when an individual in the group perceives, usually through worship, meditation or prayer, a new "call" or, as Quakers call it, a "leading." In this case, clearness is a way for the group to explore the leading with the person who feels it, test it, and consider its implications for the community and for the individual. (Additional Quaker resources on clearness and spiritual discernment are provided in Appendix II. Others are listed in the bibliography).

Clearness is neither for everyone nor for all situations. This process is certainly not appropriate for someone in need of professional counseling. It is meant for people who are essentially whole and emotionally healthy, although they may be going through a period of personal crisis. Clearness is also not meant for every decision. Routine matters do not require this kind of careful and time consuming process.

Some situations may also require other responses by a caring community. For instance, if an individual or a family is going through a period of crisis or needs to be sustained by others, the community may wish to respond by creating some kind of ongoing support mechanism, rather than a clearness committee. (Note this is different from the support groups described elsewhere in this book, in that this is one-way care for an individual or family,

---

*Loring, Patricia. *Spiritual Discernment: The Context and Goal of Clearness Committees.* Pendle Hill Pamphlet 305, p.12.

not mutual support by all members of a small group.) The decision aspects of the situation may be appropriate for clearness at some stage in the process.

We have heard of clearness being used for an amazing array of decisions. Some examples include:

> *A teenager was trying to figure out whether to complete high school. A clearness committee helped him evaluate his options and identify additional information he needed.*

> *A couple was struggling about whether to send their children to public or private schools and asked for a clearness group to meet with them.*

> *A single woman sought support in determining whether or not to have a child without a partner.*

> *A lesbian couple asked members of their community to help them decide whether to have a ceremony of commitment, similar to Quakers' use of the process for all marriages.*

> *A woman used clearness to explore how to follow a calling to travel to Russia as a spiritual support to people there.*

> *Couples have used clearness processes to help make decisions in the process of separation and divorce.*

> *An older Quaker man asked for guidance from his meeting about his vocal ministry, concerned about its source and authenticity.*

> *A couple was advised by a family therapist to place their son in a children's institution in order to deal with severe behavioral problems. A clearness group helped them make the difficult decision to go ahead—with positive results.*

> *A social scientist was moved to write and publish a book-length challenge to a development organization about their methods. He asked a clearness group to discuss his ideas, read the manuscript, and keep his intentions positive.*

> *A couple used a clearness process to decide whether to leave any of their inherited wealth to their children or to give all of their assets to social change groups before they died.*

> *A young man finished his training in an ecological field, but came very close to deciding to become a minister. In the midst of his confusion about his future direction, a clearness group from his faith community helped him decide to commit himself to environmental efforts and to see this work as his ministry.*

Clearness is a flexible tool which can be applied to many important life decisions, bringing members of our communities to stand shoulder-to-shoulder with us as we face challenges and opportunities.

FORMATS AND STYLES FOR CLEARNESS MEETINGS: THREE CASES

As a basic concept, clearness is quite simple; there is no need to codify a fixed set of rules for accomplishing it. On the other hand, we can draw on the wealth of experience with this flexible process to inform future uses and adaptations of it.

The three examples of clearness meetings which follow illustrate some of the many possible variations on the clearness process. Focus persons and facilitators are invited to read through these to get a sense of the range and to stimulate their thinking about what they want in their own clearness sessions.

Each example is accompanied by the agenda that was used for the meeting. Although these examples are based on real experiences, each is partly fictionalized or a composite of several actual cases.

Case One
Brendan Faces the Music

Brendan had been totally immersed in Central America organizing work for several years, networking among the many groups, running training programs and study groups for activists, engaging in successive action campaigns, and attending a seemingly endless series of meetings. To earn money he had been working parttime as a waiter and, occasionally, as an extra carpenter for a contractor friend. On the side, when he had time, Brendan played music and wrote songs. He was often asked to sing or lead singing at rallies and group meetings; it was a part of the movement life that he loved.

In his third year of organizing, Brendan began to realize that he was feeling resentful of the work and dreading going to yet another meeting. He didn't feel so much exhausted as uninspired and without direction. He talked with a few friends about how he was feeling. He asked his friend Casey about

60

clearness, a process he had heard about but never tried. He knew that Casey had taken part in several clearness meetings and had held one recently for himself.

Brendan thought about who might be good members of the group. He asked Casey to facilitate and invited five others: Suzanna, who had worked on several campaigns with him; Greg, his contractor friend; Jill, an activist with whom he had had a peer counseling relationship for several years, although nowadays they mostly just sat around and talked; Janey, his oldest friend from high school days; and Everett, his "music buddy" with whom he would get together and jam when they both had time.

In preparation for the meeting, Brendan wrote up his thoughts about his possible future directions. He mentioned his ambivalence about Central America organizing—commitment mixed with guilt, since there was so much more to be done there. Among his options he listed 1) continuing with work and organizing as at present; 2) going to school to get a master's degree in political science and teaching so that he could teach high school social studies; 3) going to Central America on a development project (maybe using his carpentry skills); and 4) getting a full-time job for awhile and "just chilling out." At the end of his paper he wrote, "Of course, music will have to fit in there somewhere."

The clearness group got together for a potluck dinner (everyone brought something to share) at Casey's house. Afterwards, the group assembled in the living room and, with Brendan and Everett leading, sang a few songs. Members of the group then briefly shared what was happening in their lives—a quick "check-in." Casey reviewed the agenda and talked a bit about the purpose of the meeting. "Brendan is looking for feedback about his role in the movement and how he might develop a sense of a longer-term career." He also explained the role of the clearness group. He mentioned that Jill had agreed to take some notes for Brendan, noting mainly major points and suggestions.

Casey then asked members to state any biases they might feel up front. Suzanna said, half-jokingly, "I'll kill you if you desert the Central America movement. Seriously, I think you are a key person in this area and we will miss you terribly. But we need you whole and sane and I'll support whatever you decide." Greg and Everett both shrugged and said they didn't have a particular bias. Jill said, "I only want you to decide what you want in the long term and really go for it!" Janey remarked, "I don't care what you do, so long as it makes you happy—and it wouldn't hurt to leave room for a personal relationship!"

Casey asked Brendan if he wanted to add anything to the background paper he had already distributed. Brendan thought a minute and then talked about feeling not quite an adult. "Here I am thirty-four years old and I still don't have a steady job or a family. I have been working really hard, but it feels all scattered and unreal. I am committed to reducing the suffering of people in Central America, but I don't see how we are making a difference. The only time I feel whole is when I am singing."

The group then started asking questions. Had Brendan looked into graduate programs? What were his financial resources? Was there a way to continue with organizing work, but reduce the stress? How did he feel about teenagers and teaching? What would it be like to go from the experiential training model of the movement to teaching in a high school? What kinds of full-time jobs could he get? Someone suggested two development organizations active in Central America who might welcome his skills. After about forty-five minutes, Casey called a break.

After the break, Janey asked to speak. "Brendan, something has been bothering me ever since the beginning of the meeting when you said that the only time you feel whole is when you are singing. That just leapt out at me, but I didn't know where to go with it, since it didn't seem to figure in any of these options we have been considering. I'd like us to look at what music really means to you and how it fits with these other things. I know you used to have dreams about being a powerful movement musician. Where have they gone?" Everett, a man of few words, muttered, "Yeah, right."

The mood shifted in the room. Everyone waited expectantly for Brendan to respond. Greg, sitting next to him, could see that he was having trouble and put his arm around him. Finally, with tears in his eyes, Brendan looked up at Janey, smiled and said, "Hey, old friend, you nailed me." From there, the group worked with Brendan about how to bring music into the center of his life and to connect it to his passionate concerns for social justice. They discussed how he might earn a living (carpentry with Greg's crew as a day job, think about teaching eventually...) and how to continue a commitment to Central America work, but on a different basis.

Casey asked Brendan how he was doing with all this. "Well, to tell you the truth, I'm both excited and terrified at this point. But it's great—this could really happen and I'm ready to give it a try!" Casey summarized where they had come in the meeting to that point, including things members had agreed to do. Brendan had decided to take six months to move in the direction of making music his main movement work, including three months to extricate himself from various commitments, and three months to try working full-time as a carpenter while seeking opportunities to perform in public. The clearness group agreed to get together again in six months to see how it was all going. Jill gave Brendan the notes she had been taking and said, "You might want to look at these next week and see what has already changed inside you."

After a brief evaluation, Brendan decided they should end the meeting with a rousing chorus of "I Shall Be Released."

Agenda Outline:

Opening (singing, check-in, etc.)

Agenda Review: agenda, goal, role of the group, note taker

Check for Personal Biases

Comments/Background from the Focus Person

Questions/Discussion

Break

More Questions and Discussion

Summary of Conclusions, Next Steps, Collect Notes

Evaluation

Closing (song, circle, silence, refreshments...)

Case Two
Cathy Almost Leaves

Cathy moved to San Francisco to serve as an intern with a large neighborhood youth program called Get Smart. The program works with inner city young people of all racial and ethnic groups, providing tutoring, alcohol and drug recovery groups, training in community organizing, and social analysis study groups. On occasion, Get Smart works in coalition with other organizations and service agencies on campaigns around specific issues in the community. Through these campaigns, the young people gain a lot of organizing experience.

Cathy's Asian American family had moved from Taiwan to a poor neighborhood of Boston when she was seven. They struggled financially while Cathy was growing up, but by the time she was in high school, her father had set up his own computer business. Even though it was still a sacrifice for her family, during her last two years of high school, Cathy attended a private school and won a scholarship to Wellesley. After finishing college with a degree in sociology, Cathy wanted to get some practical organizing and counseling experience before going to graduate school. The internship with Get Smart seemed just right.

Although Get Smart did not provide a formal training program for its interns, it encouraged all new staff to take part in all aspects of the program, including the organizer training program. In addition, all staff were required to be in a support group. The five interns and three newer staff members formed two such support groups, with occasional participation by one of the more experienced staff members.

After five months of the year-long internship, Cathy was miserable. She didn't feel as though she knew what she was doing. Her work assignments were vague. She felt alienated from other people in the program, frustrated with her support group, and angry over a lack of attention from her supervisor. Most of the youth involved with Get Smart were Latino, African American, and white. Only one other Asian American was involved in the organization—the bookkeeper—and Cathy had heard veiled references to the "model minority" from some of the youth and even from other staff. She had been pleased with a young women's study group she started which had been researching the role of women in the community, including interviews with women in leadership positions in community organizations and politics. But that group fizzled out when a big campaign began around the school budget.

Cathy was seriously considering quitting and going back to Boston. At a moment of high frustration she blurted all of this out to Zima, the one other intern with whom she felt some friendship. Zima just listened and nodded and occasionally said, "Humph!" When Cathy finished her outburst, Zima asked, "Well, what do you want to do about it?" Cathy didn't know. Zima said, "From what you're saying, there are a bunch of tangled issues here, and you have got an important decision to make. I once was in a group to help someone think through issues like that—it was called a clearness committee. It worked somewhat like our support group, but we focused on one person and the decision they had to make. Would that work for you?" Cathy asked for time to think about it, but the next day she told Zima she was willing to try clearness.

Zima found the old photocopied handouts from the clearness meeting in which she had taken part. She and Cathy thought about who might be good to include in the clearness group and decided to make it all women. They chose one other woman from their support group, an African American woman named Jody; Elena, the Get Smart bookkeeper; Laura, a white working-class woman and one of the older organizers from Get Smart; Mrs. Chang, an older family friend who lived nearby; and Tina, Cathy's roommate. With Zima and Cathy it was a group of seven.

Zima helped Cathy put together a short paper describing her frustrations and listing the options she was considering: 1) trying to make the Get Smart internship work; 2) finding another job in San Francisco; and 3) moving back to Boston. This statement was sent out to the members of the clearness group in advance of the meeting.

The group met in a conference room at Get Smart on a Sunday morning when no one else was there. Zima asked the members of the group to start by introducing themselves and saying why they were there. Most indicated that they were there to help think with Cathy. Jody said, "Yeah, I want to assist Cathy, but when I read her statement, I realized that some of the rest of us have the same issues. I'm here for me too." Tina joked that she wanted a happy roommate: "I want to get rid of the ghost that's been hanging out in my apartment. This is an exorcism, isn't it?"

Zima explained the rest of the agenda and reminded the group that their role was to help Cathy in her decision process and that this was not a therapy group. She asked Tina to start taking notes, but to pass the paper to someone else after some time. She asked Cathy if she wanted to add anything to the statement she had already distributed to the group. Cathy did not have much to add, but said that she had talked with her parents who hoped she would find a way to make it work in San Francisco, although they mostly wanted her back at home.

For a few minutes the women asked Cathy clarifying questions about her feelings and about the options she had listed. Zima then asked the group to brainstorm the things they saw as Cathy's strengths. She asked Cathy to name three things to start and then as people called out positive items, Zima wrote them up on large sheets of newsprint "so Cathy would have to look at them!" Among other things, the women listed: smart, dedicated, sensitive, energetic, good-looking—"no, let's face it, gorgeous," well organized, analytical.

Next, Zima instructed the group to think for a minute about their "wishes" for Cathy. After several minutes of silence while everyone thought, members of the group offered "wishes." Some of them were: "I wish Cathy felt totally at home at Get Smart." "I wish Cathy a project that is all hers." "I wish Cathy a gorgeous lover." (Laughter) "I wish Cathy to regain all of the excitement and energy she came with five months ago." "I wish Cathy to be the Queen of Asian American Youth Organizing!" "I wish Cathy a sense of connection and support every day." "I wish Cathy a challenging and realistic set of learning goals." "I wish Cathy strong roots in the Asian community." When they finished this round, the group gave a few little cheers and whoops. Someone remarked, "Wow! I guess we can quit right there!"

Smiling patiently, Zima called the group back to order and turned to Cathy. "OK, sister, what's your reaction so far? Would you like to explore one of the wishes? Where are you in this?" Cathy asked for time just to absorb the things the group had said so far. She sat and gazed at the newsprint for a few minutes and then said, "I see a theme running through several of the wishes—its about me reclaiming my Asian heritage and making that a part of my work. I guess I have been trying so hard to understand other people and their cultures, I have lost track of mine. And Get Smart is supposed to be about bringing people of all kinds together. From what Jody said at the beginning, I wonder how well supported other people feel—maybe it's not just me. Let's talk about how I might follow up on this, especially reaching back to my Asian roots and reaching out to other people more."

For a few minutes the group started probing Cathy's feelings of isolation and exploring her experiences as a new immigrant and latecomer in high school—wondering if those old feelings were affecting her ability to connect with people in the Get Smart context. Zima let this discussion go for awhile, but then noted that the point had been made and reminded the group that this was not therapy—Cathy would figure out how to deal with those issues.

After a quick break (Mrs. Chang's famous egg rolls and Laura's brownies), the group got back together and worked with Cathy on the issues of bringing Asian American youth into the Get Smart program, working on issues of stereotypes and misperceptions of the Asian community in staff and youth discussions, and building better support for learning among the interns. Mrs. Chang offered to introduce Cathy to her church, a major center in the Asian community. "Yeah, and a great source for that gorgeous lover," someone joked. Elena said she had some connections in the Asian business community which might provide financial support for cross-cultural work between Asian young people and youth of other backgrounds. Jody suggested a meeting right away among all of the interns to raise the issues of better support, supervision, and learning systems. Laura said she was excited about the prospect of increasing Get Smart's outreach to the Asian community and offered to help Cathy develop a project plan.

Toward the end of the meeting, Zima asked Cathy if she felt clearer about her directions. Cathy said, "Well, sometimes I'm a little slow about these things. This is quite a shift in thinking. I think I want to let this sift for a few days, maybe even a week, and then I'll get back to each of you to let you know what I'm going to do. But I do feel renewed excitement—and this meeting itself has brought me closer to each of you. I can feel your caring and support which I had cut myself off from before. Thanks a lot!"

Jody passed Cathy the note pad which had been circulating around the room quietly. Zima asked the group to evaluate the meeting. People's positive comments: great facilitation; Cathy was brave; good group cooperation and thinking; exciting to see the shift in Cathy's thinking; fab food!; and "when can I have a clearness meeting?" On the to-be-improved side: we could have worked more with Cathy's strengths—they just sort of hung out there; this room was impersonal and institutional; could have used more time to talk through more issues; wanted to hear more about Cathy's long-term goals as a context for this meeting. To end the meeting, Zima "confessed" that she had always wanted to be a cheerleader and this was her chance. She had the group stand in a circle and do a chant for "Cathy's team."

Agenda Outline:

Introductions (if needed) and Brief Sharing

Agenda Review: role of group, purpose, agenda, note taker

Sharing from Focus Person (additions to written statement)

Questions of Clarification

Brainstorm Strengths of Focus Person

Group "Wishes" for the Focus Person

Discussion: Focus Person Chooses a "Wish" or "Wishes" to Work with Further

Break

Continued Discussion

Summary and Next Steps, Collect Notes

Evaluation

Closing (Song, cheers, hugs, more food...)

Case Three
Anna Fights Burnout*

Anna, a Quaker woman, had been working for four years as the international coordinator of a nonviolent action group with membership dispersed around the world and demanding, crisis-prone projects in areas of hot conflict in Asia and Central America. It had been a grueling few years and Anna felt at the end of her physical, mental, and spiritual rope—yet for some reason she was reluctant to resign from the job and move on. Finally, after conversations with close friends, she decided to call a clearness meeting, something she had done at several points in her past and was quite familiar to her.

Anna gathered four people for the clearness meeting: Jim, her housemate; Judy, a co-worker; Karl, her activist lover; and Louisa, her spiritual partner, a woman with whom she often met for meditation and informal sharing. She asked Louisa to serve as clerk, or facilitator. Because the members of the group all knew Anna well and were fully informed about her dilemma, she felt that no written statement was necessary prior to the meeting.

The group gathered one February evening in a quiet cozy room with a wood stove at a local retreat center. Louisa began the meeting with a brief explanation of the steps of the process for this particular meeting. The group then settled into a period of silent worship. Out of that silence, Anna then shared a bit of the dilemma before her: her feelings of responsibility to the organization which she had worked so hard to build; her lack of clarity about her own next steps; her wish to have more time for a personal life; her strong commitment to work for peace; and her precarious financial situation. She mentioned that she was having trouble sorting out her desires for her own future from the demands of the organization's future.

For the next period, members of the group observed the discipline of only asking Anna questions. They held back their own opinions or advice and asked probing questions to help Anna clarify her own sense of direction. There was lots of silence between questions and Anna paused quietly to consider each question before answering. Jim asked what Anna really wanted in life. Judy probed for Anna's reasons for hanging on in the action organization, and where her sense of obligation came from. Karl remarked, "Anna, I have this picture of you swinging on a vine from one place to another, but afraid to let go of one vine to grasp the next. What does it feel like to consider leaving the action group? What are your worst fears?"

Louisa said, "Try just closing your eyes and imaging your future. What do you see?" Anna leaned back and closed her eyes. After a minute or so she smiled and said, "I have no idea what this means, but I get a picture of flying

---

*The format used for this clearness process is based on the process described by Jan Hoffman in her article in Appendix II.

on a winged creature of some kind." "OK, just give it more time. Sit with it another minute. What's your sense?" Louisa suggested. "I get this wonderful feeling of being carried and nurtured—real relief. I don't know where it's taking me, but it sure feels great!"

Anna was concerned about the timeline for the organization and when it might be convenient for her to leave. The next general assembly of the organization, planned for the coming September, had seemed a logical time for transition to a new coordinator, but the assembly had been postponed at least six months for financial reasons. Every time Anna contemplated continuing in the job for more than another year, she felt a huge knot well up in her stomach. She thought that she could hold out until September, but no longer.

Karl asked, "What is *your* timeline? Can you consider your needs as important as the organization's? It sounds to me as though you would like to leave by June. Why not?" Anna paused, her shoulders dropped. "Really? I could get out of this by June?! You know, I think that's what I really want, but I have not been letting myself consider that."

After further consideration, Anna said that she was clear that she should resign from the organization, effective in June. She was ready for this step, even though she was not sure where her own path would lead next, and it was not certain how the organization would find a replacement for her, given its fragile financial situation and the difficulty of finding someone willing to do an impossible job at low pay. The clearness group supported her in this "leap of faith" and helped her think about how she might discover her next "leading" (sense of direction arising from spiritual guidance).

Towards the end of the meeting, Louisa asked Anna how she wanted to use the rest of the time. Anna chose a period of open reflections (instead of more questions) to be followed by an imaging process. In the open reflection time which followed, members discussed how Anna might earn a living as she sought further guidance about her next steps. They also helped plan how she might announce her decision to leave her job, and how she might rest and recover from her near burnout. [Later, members of the clearness group and some of her friends and colleagues helped raise money to give Anna two weeks at a retreat center, as a going-away present on the occasion of her departure from the action organization.]

Louisa explained the imaging process. "The purpose is to bring other resources into the picture, beyond our intellects and words. I have found that this process taps into sometimes powerful images which then become material for further reflection by the focus person or cast some new light on the matter before us. Sometimes the person giving an image doesn't know what it means, but I find it works to just let them be and let the focus person discover a meaning eventually. The images belong to the focus person." To begin the imaging process, Louisa stood behind Anna's chair and rested her hands on her shoulders. She asked Anna if she wanted other members of the group to touch her during the process. "Sure," said Anna. The group moved in closer, Judy held one hand and Karl the other, while Jim grasped her elbow. The group settled into silent worship again and then members shared the images that came to them as they focused on Anna. Judy saw Anna floating with a big grin on her face. Karl saw tension dropping from her like sheets of water. Louisa felt warmth and light flowing from inside of Anna as she strode along a path into the future. Jim seemed uncomfortable with this part of the process, but he quietly held Anna's arm and listened to the others speak.

Before the meeting ended, Louisa again led the group into silent worship and then the meeting closed as all joined hands in a circle. Judy gave Anna the notes she had been taking.

Agenda Outline:

Facilitator (or clerk) opens the meeting, explains format and agenda steps

Period of silent worship or meditation

Sharing from the focus person: brief summary of the question or concern and brief background

Discipline of questions: members ask questions only—short, honest, probing, caring, challenging questions

Break (as needed)

More questions

Focus person's choice about how to proceed next. Some options are: silent worship or meditation with people speaking as they wish; silence, out of which people share images which come to them (optional: members physically touch the focus person); continue with more questions as above; focus person asks questions of the group; members are asked for their reflections or advice

Summary of any clarity reached from the focus person

Agreement on next steps, if any. Give notes to focus person

Closing (silence, singing, joining of hands...)

ORGANIZING A CLEARNESS PROCESS

This section is addressed to the focus person (the person initiating the clearness process), who is, therefore, the "you" addressed here.

There are several steps to setting up a clearness process: choosing a facilitator; choosing the clearness group; meeting with the facilitator; and deciding a format and style for the clearness session.

Choose a Facilitator

The focus person chooses one person to serve as facilitator (sometimes called chairperson, clerk, or convener) to guide the process. This frees you, as focus person, to give full attention to listening and responding in the meeting. As you choose a facilitator, keep in mind the following:

Is this someone who does not have a strong bias, who can keep a clear head, even if the meeting gets emotional?

Is this someone with reasonably good facilitation skills? (Does not have to be an expert).

Is the prospective facilitator someone who feels comfortable with the style of meeting you envision?

Choose the Clearness Group

Clearness groups (or committees) can be as small as three plus the focus person or as large as seven plus the focus person. You can decide the size and the kinds of balance you want in the group, based on the purpose of the meeting. Sometimes the facilitator can help you decide whom to invite. Some considerations:

Try to find a balance among people who know you well as personal friends and people who might have specific information or expertise relevant to the issues at hand.

Choose people who will be reasonably comfortable with the style of meeting you decide upon.

Do you have a friend who is a particularly good source of support, someone who is aware of how you react and knows your emotional needs? Such a person might be a valuable member of a clearness group. (Some focus persons have asked one person to participate in the meeting with the sole function of providing support to the focus person.)

For some it will be important to include a person or persons who share your spiritual perspective.

If the decision is about work or career, someone who knows you well in that area of your life might be included.

A Note on Biases

People who have a distinct bias or strong feelings about the issues or about your decision may or may not be good to have in the meeting. Biases or feelings are not necessarily a problem so long as they are acknowledged openly. Some people with emotional reactions may rule themselves out. Consider whether the person is able to think clearly about you, despite any feelings or biases. For instance, your business partner might be upset about your proposal to leave the business to pursue other dreams, but might still be able to think about whether it would be right for you. Not all parents would be helpful in a discussion of whether their unmarried daughter should have a child as she has always wanted, though some would.

Meet with the Facilitator

The focus person meets with the facilitator before the meeting to discuss several things.

Clearness Question/Problem

Clarify the question or decisions being brought to the clearness meeting. Clearness groups find it difficult to deal helpfully with a vague concern; focus the issues enough to make them manageable. If you have several issues, try to set some priorities among them or look for a unifying theme.

> *Too vague/general:* "I need to figure out my career."

> *Better:* "I want to explore several specific career options, considering how each of the options draws on my skills and engages my passionate interests."

Choosing the Clearness Group

If you have not already selected the clearness group, talk with the facilitator about what other people might be invited. Decide who will ask them to participate and notify the members of the time and place of the meeting.

Task of the Clearness Group

Identify the task of the clearness group. What are you asking of the group? Do you want the group to help you think through a decision? To give feedback? To raise questions and challenge your thinking? To generate suggestions or more options? To help resolve particular dilemmas? To offer support? To test a spiritual call or leading? Another way to approach this is to ask, "Where do you want to be at the end of the meeting?"

Meeting Style and Agenda

Discuss the style of meeting which will meet your needs and draw up a tentative agenda. Look together at the three examples provided in "Formats and Styles for Clearness Meetings" or invent your own tone and agenda.

Questions for Clearness

Look together at the next section on "Personal Preparation for Clearness." Review the section on questions for clearness and decide which of these are the important questions for your problem or dilemma. Or make up new ones. Discuss how you will provide information to group members: in writing ahead of time or in a verbal report in the meeting. (The use of large sheets of newsprint to present information in the meeting is often helpful.)

Support

Arrange for the support you will need in the meeting itself. What are points of potential difficulty? What are you afraid might happen?

Physical Setting

Decide where to have the clearness meeting—in a private space, free from interruptions (including phones!). Arrange for comfortable seating for all and, possibly, ask someone in the group to provide some kind of refreshment for the break or after the meeting.

Decide on a Style and Format for the Clearness Meeting

Clearness is an extremely flexible concept and there is room for a wide range of styles in clearness meetings.

> Political activists have had exciting and creative meetings full of social analysis and challenging thinking about the strategic use of the focus person's skills and interests.

> Those engaged in spiritual practice have held clearness meetings characterized by attention to a search for discernment based on inner spiritual guidance.

> People with an interest in issues of personal growth have included sensitive discussion of how a proposed direction might affect goals

for individual change. For instance, a group might consider how issues of fear about taking visible leadership affect the decision to accept a particular job.

These styles are not mutually exclusive. Many clearness meetings are a blend of two or more of these elements or still other styles. As focus person, you are in a position to determine what kind of meeting you want. For illustration of some of the possibilities, see the section on "Formats and Styles for Clearness Meetings."

PERSONAL PREPARATION FOR CLEARNESS

Preparation for a clearness meeting is almost as important as the meeting itself. The old saw that "what you get out of it is based on what you put into it" applies here. Once you have done the basic work to organize the clearness process, as the focus person, you begin an important part of the clarification process through reflection, considering a set of questions, and deciding what information to share with the clearness group ahead of time.

Personal Reflection

Each individual has his/her own way of reflecting about a set of personal issues. A few of the processes people use include:

Writing down thoughts/keeping a journal

Talking with friends or relatives

Taking long walks

Reading inspirational or analytical literature

Meditation/prayer

Visualization

Dream interpretation

Peer counseling

Therapy

Part of preparation consists of identifying your own process of reflection and applying it to the issue or set of issues you are bringing to the clearness process. For most people, this requires deliberately setting aside time in busy lives.

Questions for Clearness

The questions listed below are meant to stimulate thinking by the focus person before a clearness meeting. You might choose to answer some of them in a clearness statement for distribution to all members of the group prior to the meeting. Some might be useful in your process of reflection but need no direct communication to the group.

The questions purposely represent a wide variety. They certainly do not exhaust all of the possible questions. Only some are relevant to any particular clearness. You are invited (with help from the facilitator, if desired) to choose among them or to devise new ones. You might also read the section of this book on Strategic Questioning.

We suggest that you contemplate these questions one at a time. Think about each question and see if it connects to important issues for you. If so, mark it for further reflection. If not, move on.

Questions for Sorting

We have found it valuable for the focus person to sort out several important dimensions in relation to proposed directions or decisions. These dimensions tend to fall into the overlapping categories of feelings, thoughts, and inspiration or intuition.

What are your strong *feelings* about the issues before you? Is there past history which makes this question particularly difficult? Are there elements of joy? Stress? Excitement? Fear? What is your gut sense of the right way forward for you?

What is your best and most creative *thinking* about these issues? What do you think is the most logical or reasonable direction for you to take? What is your analysis of the political or social change elements of the decision?

What is your *inspiration or intuitive sense* about the issues before you? What images come to you about your future? What cherished vision do you hold about these issues? For those who practice a spiritual discipline, what arises out of your process of prayer or meditation?

Specific Questions

What elements of your personal history are relevant to the decision being made? How does that history affect you now?

What are your present commitments? How do you spend your time and how do you feel about those priorities?

What do you need in your life in order to function well and creatively? Do you pay attention to those needs?

What is holding you where you are? What is pushing you into new directions? What comes from inside you? What comes from outside you?

If you sense spiritual guidance, where is it leading you?

What are your dreams? What are the barriers you perceive to reaching them? How might you overcome those barriers?

Imagine yourself at some future event which represents your attaining some aspect of your dreams. How did you get there? "Dream backwards" from that point in the future to the present.

What are you living for? What keeps you from living fully for the things you want to live for?

What are your long- and short-term goals in terms of: family and relationships, career, social change, personal growth, spiritual life, health, geography and living situation?

What are the specific options you are considering for your future? What are the positive and negative factors you associate with each option? (Suggestion: divide a sheet of paper in two vertically and list the positives on one side and the negatives on the other for each option separately.)

What additional information do you need in order to make a good decision?

What values do you hold which bear upon this decision?

What financial issues impinge on your decision? Are there non-financial resources in your community that might help address financial issues (housing, child care, other in-kind offerings...)?

What are the implications of your proposed action or change in direction for your community, family, fellow workers, etc.?

Write Up a Clearness Statement

Writing a concise statement for clearness starts the process of focusing and clarifying for the focus person. Refining the issues and questions you have is part of this important step.

We have found that members of the clearness group prefer to get basic information about the clearness in advance, which also gives them time to ponder the issues and think about their own questions. This also gives all members of the group a consistent base of information, since all will not know you equally well or in the same contexts.

Based on your reflections, write up at least some of the background information which will be helpful to members of the clearness group and distribute the paper ahead of time. At a minimum, the written paper includes a statement of the problem, issue or dilemma, an explanation of what you want from the group, plus some background information. Providing this will save valuable time in the meeting; otherwise you will have to spend time laying out facts and considerations in the meeting itself.

Depending on the complexity of the issues involved (and the verbosity of the focus person!) we have seen clearness statements ranging from one page to ten pages. Shorter is better: part of your process of clarification will be deciding what is most important to share in writing or as introductory information in the meeting.

Timothy's Story

Timothy was seventeen and about to finish his junior year in high school. During that school year he had negotiated a special student status, attending a minimum number of classes, working on special projects, and working at an alternative school with younger children. He was at a point of trying to figure out what he should do during his senior year. In consultation with his parents and teachers, he decided to hold a clearness meeting.

Timothy and his parents asked a friend of the family familiar with the clearness process to facilitate the meeting. In addition to Timothy and his mother and father, they invited his school advisor, another teacher who knew him well, and another close adult friend to participate on the committee. Timothy considered including people his own age, but decided he was comfortable with the adults in the group and did not think any of his friends were exactly right for the process.

The facilitator met with Timothy ahead of time and helped him think about how to prepare for the meeting. They identified the main options Timothy was considering: finishing high school in a fairly conventional way; taking the year to do some interesting projects including, possibly, an internship in Washington; and attending a local community college part time while taking a GED exam for his high school diploma.

With the facilitator, Timothy decided that he would think about the positive and negative aspects of each of his options and write those up on sheets of paper for presentation to the clearness group. He would also consider his longer-term hopes and plans and how the different options might affect them. He noticed that each of the possibilities he was considering contained pulls and tugs that represented things he wanted. He would have to make some choices. Timothy also began to think about the effects of his decision on his friends, family, and the school community. These were the factors he talked about when he met with his clearness committee.

ROLE OF THE
CLEARNESS GROUP

Prophetic listening is listening to others in such a way that we draw out of them the seeds of their own highest understanding, of their own obedience, of their own vision, that they themselves may not have known were there. Listening can draw forth out of people things that speaking to them cannot.

— Elise Boulding

The members of the clearness group have a rewarding and challenging role. They must find ways to be supportive and affirmative while also raising questions forthrightly. Clearness group members strive to find a balance between open recognition of good thinking and sensitive challenges of fuzzy-headedness or false assumptions.

There are roles which members of a clearness group do not play. Clearness committees are not advice givers or therapists. As much as possible they suppress their own curiosity, their problem solving ability, and their urges to perform, to appear wise, insightful, or intelligent. What is left, then? What remains is helping the focus person remove barriers to their own seeing, listening, sensing, and thinking—and through that process discover the focus person's own clarity. Mostly, clearness group members achieve this by listening, questioning, and, at times, by remaining silent and waiting.

Clearness Group Functions

A clearness group performs several functions, some of which are discussed below.

Listen

Good listening has amazing potential for generating creative thought. One of the primary roles of the clearness group is to listen to the focus person. At times, it is useful to repeat back or paraphrase what has been heard.

"Robin, as I have listened to what you have been saying, it appears that you are most concerned about making sure that you maintain solid time with your children and that other things must take second place to that. Am I right?"

Pose Questions

Draw out the thinking and/or feelings of the focus person, prompting understanding of motivations, reasoning, or insights at a deeper level. The most helpful questions are honest, probing, caring, challenging, and open. Loaded questions, questions with built-in advocacy, or questions asked out of curiosity are generally not helpful. Use questions not to raise doubts or worries but to spark creativity and to make sure important considerations are addressed. Group members will benefit from reading Fran Peavey's section on "Strategic Questioning" in this book as they prepare for a role as loving interrogators.

Some clearness groups adopt a discipline of only asking questions for some or all of the meeting. Jan Hoffman's article in Appendix II provides a model for this.

"Dale, how might you build a career which combines your interest in environmental issues and your skills in graphic design?"

"Chris, how might you use this time of being primarily a parent to prepare for your career after you are no longer engaged in full-time parenting?"

"Mary, you spoke movingly about the image of your hands in the clay. When you close your eyes and hold that image and the question of your future as a teacher in your mind's eye at the same time, what comes to you?"

Important Note: The focus person has the right to decline to answer a question or questions, for whatever reason, stated or unstated.

Reflect Back

Members of the clearness group play a valuable role when they reflect back to the focus person things they see or hear. Group members often perceive something that the focus person does not. Members can avoid second-guessing or psychoanalyzing by maintaining an attitude of respectful inquiry.

"George, from everything that you have said, and from the note of frustration in your voice, I sense a deep desire in you to be used to your fullest potential, to make the most complete contribution that you are able to make. It seems that this is where you feel most blocked. Does that ring true to you?"

Suggest Other Options or Possibilities

At times the focus person will bring several options for future directions to the group. The group can give feedback on those, but may also generate other options not yet considered.

> *"Terry, you have been concentrating on either getting a full-time job or on seeking a large grant. How about a part-time teaching assignment at a college combined with a subsistence stipend for the organizing work you want to do?"*

Point Out False Assumptions

A clearness group can help identify motivations or assumptions which the focus person might consider discarding or altering. For instance, people often feel compelled to move in some direction in order to fulfill someone else's expectations (parents, friends, partners, lovers). Or perhaps the focus person has been pursuing a personal goal which is either unrealistic or too modest.

> *"Brendan, I would like to push you a bit on this issue about being a professional singer with a social change message. You have a great voice and a wonderful stage presence. It might take some time and effort to make it pay, but I wonder why you are relegating this passionate part of yourself to part-time hobby status."*

Consider Feelings

The group cannot resolve, remove, or deny feelings. Nor can it act as a therapist. It can, however, consider emotions as one element of the focus person's decision-making process. The group plays a role in creating an atmosphere in which feelings, even difficult ones, can be expressed openly and listened to actively. On occasion, a group member may sense emotional issues which are affecting the perspective and choices of the focus person but which remain hidden. In that case, the group member may wish to bring the issues into the open.

> *"Pat, we haven't talked much about the option of going back to school for a master's degree. Every time we touch on it you seem to back away. How do you feel about academic work or studying?"*

Take Notes

The focus person may want someone to take notes in the meeting to free the focus person to pay attention to what is being said—and to refer back to after the meeting. One person may agree to take notes for the whole meeting, or the role can be shared among several people. Be sure to get clear instructions about what kind of notes to take: just major points, questions posed, insights, or suggestions. Some focus persons use a tape recorder.

Perform Follow-up Tasks

In some instances, the group can be helpful after the clearness meeting. Members of the group might agree to perform a specific follow-up task, to find information, or to help secure needed resources. At times, the group is not finished after one session and decides to meet again. Towards the end of the meeting, the facilitator summarizes such agreements.

> *"All right, let's see. Andy, you said you would meet with Pat next week to help her develop a financial plan for the next year. Emily will be available to give phone support to Pat during her visit home. I will check with her in two months to see how things are proceeding and to figure out if the clearness group needs to meet again."*

Spirit and Intuition

For people with a religious or spiritual outlook, there will be a "third presence" in the clearness meeting. In addition to the focus person and the clearness group, a source of spiritual guidance is present. This presence is called by many names—and all share the idea that if we open ourselves to this power, our way forward will be made clear. Even for those with a distinctly nonspiritual approach, the informed hunch or insistent intuition can play an important role.

Confidentiality

In most cases, everything said by anyone in a clearness meeting is considered confidential and not to be taken out of the room unless there is an explicit agreement otherwise. If there is question or confusion about this, the group discusses it before the end of the meeting.

A Clearness Group Is Not a Support Group

Members of a clearness group agree to help with a particular set of decisions, usually meeting only one or two times. They are not necessarily able, or even the best people, to deal with longer-term support. Short-term follow-up roles are appropriate, but avoid those that might develop into ongoing support functions. If, through the clearness meeting, it appears that ongoing assistance for the focus person is needed, establish a new group *specifically for that purpose.* (Note that this kind of one-way care and assistance for a person with a particular need is different from the process of ongoing mutual support described in the Support Group section of this book—although support groups often rally to assist a member in crisis).

> *Abigail called a clearness committee after the traumatic experience of date rape, to decide whether to press criminal*

*charges. Among others, the clearness group included two lawyers
and a therapist, all concerned but extremely busy people. After the
clearness meeting, as Abigail proceeded with the court case, her
friend Jean, who had also participated in the clearness session,
helped her set up a support group, friends who literally stood by her
through every step of the agonizing legal process.*

ROLE OF THE FACILITATOR

In addition to the roles described in "Organizing a Clearness Process," the facilitator serves a number of functions during the actual meeting.

Facilitation

The facilitator plays the usual group process roles: introducing the agenda, watching time, encouraging relatively equal participation by all members of the group, watching group energy and the need for breaks. The facilitator does not control the process but helps the group decide what it wants to do, remaining particularly sensitive to the needs of the focus person.

Attention to the Focus Person

Throughout the meeting, the facilitator maintains close communication with the focus person, asking, "Are you getting what you need from the group?" It is possible for the focus person to become overwhelmed—by the amount of ideas generated, by challenges from the group, by certain kinds of critical or negative feedback, or by the feelings associated with the decisions involved. If the facilitator senses that the group has gone beyond the ability of the focus person to absorb what is being said, it may be wise to call for a break or some other shift in focus. However, if important issues are being raised, return to them when the focus person is ready (that is, don't avoid issues just because they are difficult). The facilitator also monitors the group, noting when individual agendas or biases enter the discussion in a destructive manner.

Keeping the Group on Track

By meeting with the focus person before the meeting, the facilitator knows the what the focus person wants from the clearness. One role of the facilitator is to keep this goal in mind. At the same time, clearness groups often head off in unexpected and rich directions to great benefit. When this happens, the facilitator must judge whether this is a distracting tangent or an important area to explore. The facilitator can pose the dilemma to the group and the focus person and ask them to decide how to proceed.

Decision Making

In most cases, the decision is really in the hands of the focus person and the group's role is to assist that process. On occasion, however, the group may be asked to make a decision as a group.

When they must make a group decision, most clearness groups use a consensus model of decision-making. The facilitator guides the group towards an agreement. Normally, after some discussion and exploration of options, the facilitator will test for consensus by stating what appears to be an emerging proposal, asking the group to agree or disagree. At this point, group members might indicate that they support the proposed direction, or they might suggest changes in the proposal. Some might actually disagree. Discussion and attempts at consensus continue until the facilitator is able to state a proposed decision to which all can agree (even if some continue to have reservations). Note: A facilitator who is confused or lacks ideas can ask for a proposal or statement of consensus from other members of the group. (For more on the consensus process, see "What Makes Groups Work" in the Support Group section of this book and various resources listed in the bibliography.)

Process Notes

Most elements of the clearness meetings described in "Formats and Styles for Clearness Meetings" are self-explanatory. The following notes are offered to help facilitators (and focus persons) plan meetings.

Opening or Gathering

An opening activity is used to help a group gather and focus. In groups where people do not know each other ahead of time, some form of introduction may be most appropriate. Other ideas include sharing on a specific topic, meditation or silence, and singing. Openings (and closings) are not meant to be ritualistic, although many communities have activities they enjoy doing together regularly, which are part of their life together.

Closing

Closings provide a group ending to the meeting before people depart. Many of the same activities which are appropriate for openings can be used as closings. Some other forms of closing include: each person sharing something he/she is looking forward to; standing in a circle holding hands; and quick affirmations of the focus person or the members of the group.

Check-in

A check-in can be used as a gathering exercise. The purpose of a check-in is to provide a way for people to become fully present in the meeting, by sharing very briefly whatever they need to. This may be things going on that day or over several weeks or months. In a sense each person says, "This is what is happening in my life. Now I am going to set all of that aside and focus on the meeting." A check-in is also a way for group members to get to know each other. For a full description see "Checking-In" in the Support Group section of this book.

Bias Check

Members of the clearness group often have close personal ties to the focus person and, possibly, a personal stake in the decision being made. They may have strong feelings or prejudices about "what the focus person should do" or "what the most sensible future direction is." The bias check is an opportunity to state these feelings openly early in the meeting, so that they do not subvert the process. It is not necessary to judge or even discuss the biases people reveal, only to listen in order to understand their perspective.

Affirmations

Because clearness meetings typically involve puzzling decisions and difficult emotions, it is helpful to balance that struggle. Expressing affirmations of the focus person is one way to do that. Various methods can be used, depending on the wishes of the focus person. Some groups simply brainstorm a list of strengths while someone writes them up on newsprint. Others put a large piece of paper on the wall and ask members of the group to write strengths, gifts, and/or assets on it. Telling quick stories which illustrate the focus person's positive attributes is another way.

Evaluation

Through evaluating the meeting, we provide an opportunity to learn and improve the process. The facilitator can ask, "What worked well for people?" After members of the group have listed those positive elements (brainstorm style, without debate or commentary), the facilitator might ask, "What might have been better?" As people list those points of difficulty, the facilitator can also ask for positive suggestions for the future. Again, it is not necessary for the group to agree to any of these suggestions; they are offered for everyone's consideration.

> In the evaluation, John said, "I had a hard time listening to Karen shouting and crying. I didn't know the group would have to deal with feelings like that." The facilitator asked the group to come up with suggestions for how to handle that in the future. "The focus person or facilitator could warn the members that such

feelings are likely to come up and let people who are uncomfortable step outside during that portion of the meeting." "The facilitator could check with group members to see how they are doing. Maybe reassure them that the expression of feelings is fine." "If you know ahead of time that such feelings will come up, someone in the group could be designated to provide particular attention to emotional issues, so that the other members can relax somewhat."

A FINAL WORD:
SURPRISING OUTCOMES

I have found that something uncanny happens in clearness meetings. When the group maintains a respectful, listening, caring approach, and when the group and the focus person are in tune with each other, they encounter moments when there is an almost palpable shift—in perspective, in feeling, in the sense of what is most important. Factors find a new alignment in sometimes surprising ways. Clarity usually flows from those moments. Not always right away; emerging clearness often takes time to season fully.

I have also experienced clearness meetings where the group and the focus person went away frustrated and less clear than when they began the process. In some of those cases, though, when the group came back for a second meeting, and the right question was posed, or perhaps the needed silence and waiting was allowed, the unexpected surfaced and new creativity emerged. When a group works well, they achieve a wonderful magic and chemistry which can lead to new connections among the members.

In my experience, the phenomenon of the uncanny shift can occur in sessions conducted with a fairly intellectual and political tone as well as in sessions characterized by deep spiritual searching. The key seems to be listening profoundly—to the focus person's words, to the wordless passions that lie beneath the surface, to the personality and spirit struggling to find true expression—and thereby drawing out the focus person's own wisdom and integrity.

Section III

STRATEGIC QUESTIONING

by Fran Peavey

STRATEGIC QUESTIONING

An Approach to Creating Personal and Social Change

> Three angels come to me in the morn.
> One asks, "What are your visions? What are your concerns?"
> The second asks, "What will it take for you to do what is yours to do?"
> And the third asks, "What support will you need?"
> And my heart's angel draws herself up to her own fullness
>   feeling the wind blowing on her sails
>   and answers, "I will do my part small though it may be."
> One who asks questions cannot avoid answers.
>
> — Fran Peavey, January 1994

What we know of life is only where we have decided to rest with our questioning. We can operate with what we know—and we can be sure of one thing—somewhere someone is not resting at that state of knowing. They are researching and questioning—working on a new discovery.

We approach problems within a constantly changing body of information about the issues at stake. The amount of information that is known by human beings now doubles every five years! Very few people can keep up with the overwhelming avalanche of data being generated in any field. And changes within any body of information are so substantial and complex, even computer databases are out of date quickly.

This rapid turnover of knowledge in every field requires a new understanding of information and the way that questions relate to problems. Seeing information as a static thing, something that can be contained in an encyclopedia, is an outmoded view. A better metaphor in the 1990s is that information is like a river. In the river of information, ideas and relationships are constantly changing. Dipping into the river one day brings up different

90

perspectives than the next day, because the river has moved on with one more day of experience and thinking.

So it is with questioning. Asking the same question today elicits a different answer than yesterday. What we did not know yesterday, we may know today. Whether we have learned new information or have simply created a solution from our own synthesis and analysis, both the question and answer have changed.

Is anything ever fully known? You find one piece of information and from that piece of information new questions arise and you dip into the river again. So it goes on—discovery, new questions, new discovery, and new questions and on and on.

We can find power in approaching a problem with the feeling of "I don't know." There is also power in allowing doubt into what you think you already know. It doesn't have to be a threat to one's status or professionalism. Such an attitude, rather, allows the questions to emerge and new discoveries to begin. Such an attitude opens the door to new possibilities and may invite others with fresh resources and perspectives to create new solutions with you. It opens the door to the river of information that is flowing around the issues at stake, and helps us move into a dynamic relationship with this river and with life. *

A Special Type of Question

Questioning is a basic tool for rebellion. It breaks open the stagnant, hardened shells of the present, opening up options to be explored.

Questioning reveals the profound uncertainty that is imbedded deep in all reality beyond the facades of confidence and sureness. It takes this uncertainty towards growth and new possibilities.

Questioning can change your entire life. It can uncover hidden power and stifled dreams inside of you . . . things you may have denied for many years.

---

*My friend Mark Burch has helped me see that there are two kinds of communication. Communication of the *first* kind is about what is. It usually involves the transmission of information in a static or passive way. There is an assumption of inertia in the communication. "Things will stay the same." Communication of the *second* kind is focused on what reality could be. It creates information rather than communicating information that is already known. Mark Burch describes this as the "immersion of the person in a vibrating, tingling, undulating ocean of 'transactions.'" (*Depth Psychology and Sustainable Development*, an unpublished paper by Mark Burch, August 1991.) I see strategic questioning as an important skill in the development of this communication of the *second* kind.

Questioning can change institutions and entire cultures. It can empower people to create strategies for change.

Asking a question that leads to a strategy for action is a powerful contribution to resolving any problem.

Asking questions that open up more options can lead to many unexpected solutions.

Asking questions that help adversaries shift from their stuck positions on an issue can lead to acts of healing and reconciliation.

Asking questions that are unaskable in our culture at the moment can lead to the transformation of our culture and its institutions.

Asking questions and listening for the strategies and ideas embedded in people's own answers can be the greatest service a social change worker can give to a particular issue.

Strategic questioning is the skill of asking the questions that will make a difference.* It is a powerful and exciting tool for social and personal change. I have found it a significant service to any issue because it helps local strategies for change emerge.

Strategic questioning involves a special type of question and a special type of listening. Anyone can use strategic questions in their work and in their personal lives to liberate friends, coworkers, and political allies and adversaries to create a path for change.

Strategic questioning is a process that may change the listener as well as the person being questioned. When we open ourselves to another point of view, our own ideas will have to shift to take into account new information, new possibilities, and new strategies for resolving problems.

What would our world be like if every time we were listening to a gripe session, someone would ask, "I wonder what we can do to change that situation?" then listened carefully for the answers to emerge, and then helped that group to begin to work for change? What would it be like for you to do that in your work, family, or social context? Your attention and context might shift from a passive to an active one. You could become a creator, rather than a receiver, of solutions. This shift in perspective is one of the key things that

---

*I didn't invent the words "strategic questioning," although I thought I did. I had been using the term for four years when a few years ago, while doing some research, I came upon a small book about teaching called *Strategic Questioning* written by Ronald T. Hyman, a close friend of a college professor of mine. So I must have heard the words twenty-five years ago and the word seeds got planted way back there in my mind; then when I needed them they came blossoming up. Thank you, Ronald T. Hyman.

people need in our world just now. And the skill of asking strategic questions is a powerful contribution to making such a shift.

Were you ever taught how to ask questions? Were you ever encouraged to ask questions where the answers are not already known? Have you ever been taught about asking questions that will really make a difference? Most of us who were brought up in traditional families or in a traditional education system were not. Traditional schooling was based on asking questions to which the answers were already known: How many wives did Henry VIII have? What color is that car? What is four times five? We learned that questions have finite and "correct" answers, and that there is usually one answer for each question. The wrong answer is punished with a bad grade. The landscape of learning was divided into "right" and "wrong."

This may be a convenient way of running schools and testing people's capacity for memory in examinations but it has not been a very empowering learning process for students, or a good preparation for the questions that come up in life.

In some families, children are taught that to ask a question without a known answer is to be avoided because it makes people uncomfortable. Adults or parents who are supposed to be in charge of things seem to hate saying, "I don't know." It may even be true that asking embarrassing questions, or in any way threatening the power of adults, is a punishable offense. The child learns to stop questioning before the unknowns are revealed.

All this is unfortunate given our times, because in the 1990s—in our personal, professional, and public lives—we are surrounded with questions that have no immediately knowable answers. And if you haven't been taught how to work with such situations and how to ask questions, then this unknown landscape can intimidate and provoke fear. Learning how to ask strategic questions is a path I've created of transforming passive and fearful inquiry about the world into a dynamic exploration of the information around us and the solutions we need. We can "make up" answers to almost any problem.

Take the traditional school. What would it have been like if when the teacher asked, "What is four times five?" and we had said, "Twenty-nine," the teacher had not said "Wrong!" and left it at that, but she asked us to explain our thought process and how we got twenty-nine. We would have learned about ourselves and our thinking process and we might have discovered mathematics in an active way. The teacher might have learned something about increasing the effectiveness of her teaching methods.

In families that don't encourage questioning, an adult rarely follows up an "I don't know" with a "How can we find out?" Often they are so absorbed by their embarrassment that they do not show the child how to find out. But it is important for children to grow up knowing that doubt, uncertainty, and unknowing exist in the adult world—a world that they will inherit and need to play their part in creating solutions for.

Shaping a strategic question involves seven key features:

1. A strategic question creates motion

Most of the traditional questions that we've been taught to ask are static. Strategic questions ask, "How can we move?" They create movement. They are dynamic rather than allowing a situation to stay stuck.

Often the way a conversation is structured creates resistance to movement. The martial art t'ai chi teaches a lot of wisdom about meeting resistance. It says that when you meet an obstacle, you only make it more firm by pushing directly on it. If you meet an object coming at you with resistance, it is not very useful at all. T'ai chi says that if you meet and move with the energy of the obstacle coming at you, taking the energy from the other, then motion in a new direction emerges. Both parties end up in a different place than where they started, and the relationship between them is changed.

This same shift in a new direction happens when you ask a strategic question. As an example, suppose Sally is working on where she will live, and perhaps she has heard of some good real estate bargains in Sydney, and she's a bit stuck on what she should do next. I could say to her, "Why don't you just move to Sydney?" This question might be provocative, but is not very helpful. Really it's a suggestion pretending to be a question. For my own reasons I think she should move to Sydney. Perhaps I am projecting into the question my own wish to move to Sydney. Whatever my reasons I'm leading her because I am asking a manipulative question, and it is likely that the more I pressure Sally, the less likely she is to consider the Sydney option.

A more strategic question would be to ask Sally, "What type of place would you like to move to?" or "What places come to mind when you think of living happily?" or "What is the meaning of this move in your life?" Sally is then encouraged to talk about the qualities she wants from her new home, to set new goals. You can then work with her to achieve these goals.

Asking questions that are *dynamic* can help people explore how they can move on an issue. On my first working trip to India with the Friends of the Ganges project, I asked the local people, "What would you like to do to help clean up the river?" Now, you might ask, "How did I know they wanted to clean up the river?" Well, I wanted to ask a question that assumed motion on this issue. I assumed that people are always wanting to do more appropriate behavior. I further assumed that they wanted to move from their state of powerlessness regarding what to do about the pollution in the Ganges. Many interesting ideas emerged when I used that question—some of which we have implemented.

When we are stuck on a problem, what keeps us from acting for change is either a lack of information, or that we have been wounded in our sense of personal power on an issue, or that there is no system in place that enables us to move the issue forward. In our stuckness, we don't see how to make the motion. When I ask a question like, "What would you like to do to help clean up the river?" I open up a door for the local people to move beyond their grief, guilt, and powerlessness about the pollution to active dreaming and creating of their own contributions.

2. A strategic question creates options

If I asked Sally, "Why don't you move to Sydney?" I have asked a question that is dynamic only in one direction (Sydney). It very much limits the options she is challenged to think about. A more powerful strategic question opens the options up. "Where would you like to live?" or "What are the three or four places that you feel connected to?" These are much more helpful questions to ask her at this time. Sally might have been so busy thinking about the real estate bargains in Sydney that she has lost a sense of all the other possibilities and her real goals.

A strategic questioner would help Sally look at the many options equally. Supposing Sally says she could move to Byron Bay or Sydney. It's not up to me to say to myself, "I think Sydney is the best, and I should encourage her down that path." If you're being ethical about it, then you could best help Sally sort out her own direction by questioning all the options evenhandedly, with the same enthusiasm and interest in discussing both Sydney and Byron Bay. Not only that, but you could help by asking if any more options occur to her during the questioning time (Twin Falls, Idaho . . . or New Plymouth, New Zealand). Out of these questions, a new option may emerge.

It is particularly important for a strategic questioner not to focus on only two options. We are so accustomed to binary thinking, whether it's either Sydney or Byron Bay . . . that Brisbane cannot emerge as a viable alternative. Usually when someone is only considering two options, they simply have not done the creative thinking to look at all the possibilities. People are usually comfortable when they have two options and think they can make a choice at that level. This "choice" is part of the delusion of control. And since two alternatives are already more complex than one, people stop thinking. Though the world is far more complex and exciting than any two options would indicate, having two options creates the idea that a choice, however limited, is being made.

I have a friend whose daughter got into some trouble and ran away. My friend was fortunate in that she knew which train her daughter was probably leaving on in a few hours' time. She was trying to decide whether to just let the daughter get on the train and run away, or to go to the train and insist that she come home. I talked it over with her, and we worked on these options for a while, and then I asked, "What else could you do to help your daughter with her conflicts?" She thought and then a new idea came up. She could run away *with* her daughter, and take the twelve hours on the train to help her sort things out. Now, because my friend was scared and afraid for her daughter, she had been unable to think of this fine option until the door was opened through the question. It was the kind of option that she might have thought of when all her anxious feelings had subsided.

3. A strategic question digs deeper

Questions can be like a lever you use to pry open the stuck lid on a paint can. And there are long-lever questions and short-lever questions. If I have just a short lever, we can only just crack open that lid on the can. But if we have a longer lever, or a more dynamic question, we can open that can up much wider and really stir things up.

Some people approach problems with their heads just like a closed paint can. If the right question is applied, and it digs deep enough, then we can stir up all the creative solutions to that problem. We can chip away a lot of the crusty sediment that is trapping the lid on that person's head. A question can be a stirrer. It can lead to synthesis, motion, and energy.

4. A strategic question avoids "Why"

When I asked Sally, "Why don't you move to Sydney?" it was a question that focused on why she doesn't do it, rather than creating a more active and forward motion on the issue. Most "why" questions are like that. They force you to defend an existing decision or rationalize the present. "Why" questions also have the effect of creating resistance to change.

The openness of a particular question is obvious at the gross extremes, but becomes far more subtle and subjective as you deepen your understanding of the skills of strategic questioning. For example, can you feel the difference between asking, "Why don't you work on poverty?" and, "What keeps you from working on poverty?" Sometimes a "Why" question is very powerful as you focus on values, and meaning. But in general it is a short-lever question.

5. A strategic question avoids "yes or no" answers

Again, these type of questions ("Have you considered . . .") don't really encourage people to dig deeper into their issues. A question answered with a "yes" or "no" reply almost always leaves the person being asked in an uncreative and passive state. A strategic questioner rephrases their queries to avoid the dead end of a "yes" or "no" reply. It can make a huge difference to the communication taking place.

I heard of a student who was very intrigued by the ideas behind strategic questioning. He realized that he hardly ever spoke a question to his wife without getting simply a "yes" or "no" in reply. A week after the class on strategic questioning, he reported that the technique had completely changed his home life! He had gone home and told his wife about these special types of questions, and they agreed to avoid asking a question that has a "yes" or "no" answer for a week. He reported they had never talked so much in their lives!

6. A strategic question is empowering

A strategic question creates the confidence that motion can actually happen, and this is certainly empowering. When I asked people in India, "What would you like to do to clean your river?" it assumes that they have a part in that picture of healing. It even expresses a confidence in the person being questioned that they have a contribution to designing the cleaning-up process.

One of my favorite questions is, "What would it take for you to change on this issue?" This question lets the other person create the path for change. Imagine an environmental protester going to a lumber mill owner and asking, "What would it take for you to stop cutting down the old-growth trees?" This question is an invitation to the mill owner to cocreate options for the future of his business *with* the community. The owner might tell the questioner the obstacles he faces in making changes to his business, and maybe they can work together to satisfy some of their mutual needs so that the old-growth trees can be preserved. The planning that comes out of asking such a strategic question may not exactly resemble what either party wanted in the beginning, but a new reality is born out of the dialogue and could well work to achieve both the protester's and the mill owner's goals.

Empowerment is the opposite of manipulation. When you use strategic questioning, rather than putting ideas into a person's head, you are actually allowing that person to take what's already in their head and work with it.

I had a student who worked in the command structure of a large police force. Like many government departments, his department had been restructured, and this change led to stress and disgruntlement among colleagues. They were not working together as a team. For weeks in their staff meetings, members of the department had been asking themselves, "What is wrong with the way we are working?"

When my student took the strategic questioning method back to his unit, his department started to approach their difficulties with different, more empowering questions. They asked, "What will it take for us to function as a team?" "How do we want to work together?" "What do each of us want to do?" "What support do we each need?" They reported that after the strategic questioning session, the low morale started to improve, meetings became creative, and a sense of teamwork returned to the unit.

7. A strategic question asks the unaskable questions

For every individual, group, or society, some questions are taboo. And because those questions are taboo they wield tremendous power. A strategic question is often one of these "unaskable" questions. And it usually is unaskable because it challenges the values and assumptions that the whole issue rests upon.

I like the fairy tale about the emperor who walked in a parade without any clothes on because he had been tricked by some unscrupulous weavers into thinking he was wearing a magnificent costume. It was a child that asked the unaskable question, "Why doesn't the emperor have any clothes on?" If that child had been a political activist, she might have asked other unaskable questions, such as, "Why do we need an emperor?" or "How can we get a wiser government?"

In the early 1980s, one of the unaskable questions for me was, "What shall we do if a nuclear bomb is dropped?" You couldn't answer that without facing our overwhelming capacity for destruction, and the senselessness of it. That question allowed many of us to move beyond terror and denial, and work politically to keep that destruction from happening.

Some other unaskable questions might be: for the seriously ill person, "Do you want to live or die?" For those involved in sexual politics: "Is gender a myth?" For the workaholic: "What do you do for joy?" For the tree activist: "How should we make building materials?" Or for the politician: "What do you like about the other party's platform?" or "How could both parties work together more closely?"

Questioning values is a strategic task of our times. This questioning is important because it is the values behind highly politicized issues that have usually brought us into the trouble in the first place. We need to look at a value, a habit, an institutional pattern, and ask, "How is this value functioning in my own life?" "In what ways do these values work for and against the common good?" "Are these values pro-survival (pro-life) or anti-life?" If you can ask the unaskable in a nonpartisan way, not to embarrass someone but to probe for more suitable answers for the future, then it can be a tremendous service to anyone with an issue on which she or he is "stuck."

Question Families

All questions differ in their power. They differ in the depth they take a person to and they differ in their dynamic quality through time. A question can be more or less dynamic, more or less strategic, more or less action-creating, longer- or shorter-levered.

To adapt Edward de Bono's terms, there are "rock" questions, those that assume a tough truth, which focus on hard-edged, permanent, unchanging reality; and then there are "water" questions, which are those that flow, that work to find a way through, a reality that moves, a focus on "to" rather than "is." A water question takes the form of the container into which it is poured, but is not a form unto itself.

I like to think of these question families as increasing in fluidity, dynamism, and strategic power as you go down from level to level. In any use of the strategic questioning process, we would start near the top of the family order and work our way down to the more powerful question families.

The First Level—Describing the Issues or Problems

While this level does not use strategic questions as such, describing the issue or problem is an important job. We need to gain the facts and points of view of all the main players in order to frame the strategic questions later.

1. Focus Questions

These questions identify the situation and the key facts necessary to an understanding of the issues at stake. When using questioning with an individual, this is the time when the facts of the situation are presented. Questions here focus on understanding the relevant parts of their story. When using strategic questioning in a community-polling process, questions focus on how the people in the community think about the particular issue at stake.

The key in framing the questions is to be open and nonpartisan in both the questions and in the tone of the questioner. It should be an equally valid question for a person no matter what their position is on the issue.

"What aspects of our community life concern you?"

"What do you think about the logging of old-growth redwoods?"

"How has the violence in our community affected you?"

"What are you most concerned about in your community?"

2. Observation Questions

These questions are concerned with what you see and the information you have heard regarding the situation.

"What do you see?"

"What do you hear?"

"What have you heard and read about this situation?"

"Which sources do you trust and why?"

"What effects of this situation have you noticed in people, in the earth?"

"What do you know for sure and what are you not certain about?"

3. Analysis Questions

These questions focus on the meaning given to events. Here the questioner is trying to ascertain how a person thinks about the situation, what motivation is ascribed to key participants in the story, and the relation of individuals and events. "Why" questions are appropriate here. You are still gathering information and your questions usually create little motion—but you might be surprised. Sometimes these questions trigger strong feelings, or unanticipated motion.

"What do you think about . . . ?"

"What are the reasons for . . . ?"

"What is the relationship of . . . to . . . ?"

4. Feeling Questions

These questions are concerned with body sensations, emotions, and health. It is important not to skip over these questions. Feelings often interfere with thinking, trust, and imagination. Listening to and honoring the personal consequences of an event or issue is important in freeing the person to think about the area.

You do not have to "fix" the feelings; you can't. Simply listen respectfully and, when you sense the person is ready, move on. They may return to this level from time to time naturally. Some people may wish to spend very little time in the feeling level, while others may get lost in feeling and need some encouragement to move into a more dynamic discussion.

"What sensations do you have in your body when you think or talk about this situation?"

"How do you feel about the situation?"

"How has the situation affected your own physical or emotional health?"

The Second Level:
Digging Deeper by Asking Strategic Questions

Now we start asking questions that increase the motion. The mind takes off, creating new information, synthesizing, moving from what is known into the realm of what could be. Here you find more long-lever questions.

5. Visioning Questions

These questions are concerned with identifying one's ideals, dreams, and values. Articulating dreams and visions makes them a bit more real and their power is undeniable. We begin to build a bridge from the anchor of the present into midair. We stop pushing things as they are and focus on how things can develop.

"How would you like it to be?"

"What is the meaning of this situation in your own life?"

6. Change Questions

These questions are concerned with how to get from the present situation toward a more ideal situation. As future alternatives take form they are examined. Often the vision is partial but people are able to identify pieces that need to change. Later these specifics can be worked into a cohesive whole. Some people prefer a visioning process before asking specific change questions.

> "How could the situation be changed for it to be as you would like it?"
>
> "What will it take to bring the current situation toward the ideal?"
>
> "What exactly needs to change here?"
>
> "How might those changes come about? Name as many ways as possible."
>
> "What are changes you have seen or read about?"
>
> "How did those changes come about?" (Here you are trying to find the individual's "change view," which will greatly impact the strategies for change available to the person.)

7. Considering All the Alternatives

These questions examine the alternatives that come from the vision and ways things need to change. There are many ways to get to any goal. If a person is only examining two alternatives, maybe more feeling work needs to be done. Be sure not to give more time, enthusiasm, or focus to any one alternative even if you think it is the best. Also search out alternatives that seem on first glance to be odd or unusual. These ideas may have the seeds of other more viable alternatives, or suggest other ideas later on. You may focus on creating alternative visions or alternative ways of achieving the changes mentioned above. Some people will get overwhelmed with questions that ask for "all the ways" but will continue to create if you simply request more ideas one at a time. Stay open to new ideas popping up throughout the process.

> "What are all the ways you can think of that would accomplish these changes?"
>
> "How could you reach that goal? What are other ways?"
>
> "Be sure to tell me if other ideas come up."

8. Consider the Consequences

Explore the consequences of each alternative. Conscientiously examine each alternative for personal, environmental, social, or political consequences, giving the same amount of time and energy to each alternative. Returning to feeling questions may be beneficial here.

> "How would your first alternative affect the others in your group?"
>
> "What would be the effect of using the runoff for your garden?"
>
> "How would you feel doing (name each alternative)?"

"What would be the political effect if you did . . . ?"

9. Consider the Obstacles

Each alternative has things blocking its achievment. Identify the obstacle, and how to deal with it if the alternative were selected. Focusing on obstacles is an important first step in removing them. Obstacles may be addictions, values, or needs. I find it more useful to focus on what keeps a person, group, or institution from changing rather than to pressure them to change. Choices are clearest when the change and the obstacles to change are visible to both the questioner and questionee.

"What would need to change in order for alternative "a" to be done?"

"What keeps you from doing . . . ?"

"What prevents you from getting involved?"

10. Personal Inventory and Support Questions

These questions are concerned with identifying one's interests, potential contribution, and the support necessary to act. An important aspect of encouraging change is identifying the support needed to make the change. It may be financial, verbal or emotional support that is needed.

"How can I support you?"

"What would it take for you to participate in the change?"

"What do you like to do that might be useful in bringing about these changes?"

"What aspects of the situation interest you the most?"

"What support would you need to work for this change?"

At this point in the questioning a decision may begin to emerge. Check to see if the person you are questioning perceives the decision arriving. If the decision is not apparent do not force it. Often several days of pondering and several nights of dreaming are needed before clarity comes.

"Do you feel a clear decision coming forth?"

11. Personal Action Questions

These questions get down to the specifics of what to do, and how and when to do it. The actual plan begins to emerge. A questioning relationship may use several time periods to advantage. Sleeping and dreaming help the inner sense "true" the vision and plan. Action questions can also focus on alternative plans and possible outcomes in both the long and short term. Feel free to play with the planning process—remembering that the future is always changing.

"Who do you need to talk to?"

"How can you join a group that is working on this?"

"How can you get others together to work on this?"

A Special Type of Listening

An important task of strategic questioning is to create an environment where people can see the solutions that are within themselves. You listen deep into the moving heart of the person opposite you. A strategic questioner listens for the latent solutions hidden within every problem. And this involves a special type of listening. You are not merely passively listening. You are creating an action path with your attention.

This dynamic listening is in itself a special type of communication. It involves immersing yourself within the sea of "transactions" that surround an issue. You are not just listening to this information in a static or passive way. Your attention is focused on the reality of now and also you are paying attention to the clues of what now could become.

It is this dynamic listening that opens doorways within the issues being discussed. Your attention creates space around the speaker—space within which they can explore their own options.

For me, dynamic listening is more like *looking* than listening. Usually when you listen you hear everything around you in one total "hearing." But the kind of listening I am talking about is listening in only one direction—your ears are turned only toward the deepest part of the person or people opposite you. You are listening to their thinking, to their feeling, to their dreams, and to their essence. Your ears wander in between their words, their sighs, and their questions, searching out meaning, resolve, motion, and need.

You look for the obstacles to caring, the blocks to action.

You look for what is pushing people, and why they feel compelled to do something about the issue.

You look for the group's ideas of how they want things to be—how they see things could or should change.

You look for how they think about change and how change happens in their lives.

You look for the path to change that the group sees—however dimly and timidly they see it. Sometimes you explore the path together, asking questions that allow the questioner and the person answering to think freshly and creatively.

You look for the dreams and goals planted deep in the person's or group's heart.

You look for how to remove the resistance that is found on the path of change.

You look for feelings as they anticipate each possible choice or option in front of them.

You look for what support each person would need to move on any path of change.

Usually our minds are not full of attention. While we are hearing the other person speaking, our thoughts are full of reactions, distractions, fantasies, and judgments. My friend Karen Hagberg is a musician, who has written eloquently about the importance of dynamic listening. She notes:

> Without careful listening, a pianist cannot understand the various ways a single note can be played. It seems impossible that we do not listen to ourselves, what else is there to do while we are practicing?
>
> What else are we doing? There are many things, actually, that I am able to do instead of listening. I can hear an imaginary pianist, Horowitz for example, and imagine his sound as mine. I can feel the music instead of listening to it and move around a lot as I play, imagining that my feelings must be coming out as sound.
>
> Possibly I am daydreaming, half asleep, not concentrating. Usually, though, I am merely thinking about something. Thinking is not listening, nor is judging the performance as it evolves. Listening is listening.*

At times we truly listen—usually when we sense ourselves to be in danger. We stop in our tracks, our ears prick up, and we listen as if our lives depended on it. The listening required for strategic questioning is like that: we need to listen as if someone's life depends on it—because it does.

Through this dynamic listening to ourselves, to the earth, and to our fellow citizens—even those we might consider our adversaries—we may create the space where people can discover themselves, offer great ideas, or find the energy and will to make changes happen in their lives.

Questioning and Social Change

Strategic questioning is political because it is a process that encourages people to find their own way through the rapids of change. It is political because it leads to strategies for change. It is political because it can take

---

*Karen Hagberg's *Matsumoto News*, from the forthcoming book *When the Teacher is Ready the Student Appears.*

political debates beyond dogma and ideology into fresh perspectives on common problems. It is political because it is a way of transforming your attachment to your own goals and opening up options that are common goals.

It is funny how we resist change, resist participating in the changes necessary in our time. I know I do. But when we get involved with change, we can tap into a surprising stream of aliveness, creativity, and inner wisdom that is our contribution to the process of social change.

Many things keep us from acting on what we know:

> We don't know any alternatives, as we have a lack of good information on the situation.

> We may lack leadership or the confidence to pursue our goals as leaders ourselves.

> We may subscribe to a kind of fatalism that does not encourage thinking about alternatives.

> We may have taken in the often frightening information about the problem in a passive and alienating way. (Television is a prime example of passive information transfer.) And we are stuck in inactivity until our feelings about the information are dealt with.

Strategic questioning helps us break through this sort of gridlock. Dynamic dialogue focuses on how change can happen, and with it comes the potential for new "will" to arise also. In Hindi there is a special word, *sunculp*, for this will or determination. *Sunculp* is the process of tapping into the strength and collective will of the whole. It is a will that is not individual but is part of the will of the entire context. It is a resolve and commitment that we experience for the whole society. *Sunculp* can be found in any timid person through strategic questioning. The will to work for positive goals is never entirely crushed in a person or in a society although it can be impaired by oppression. However, *sunculp* is always waiting for opportunities to grow and blossom. Some years ago the prevalent view in social change work opined that if we only got the information to the "people" about what was wrong then they would make the changes necessary. Now we realize that information is simply not enough. We actually have to facilitate the *motion* on the issue and create and sustain the *sunculp* to make the change required by the information.

Here are several things to consider when shaping your questions for social change work:

Let the ideas emerge from the people affected.
Where will great social change ideas come from? One of the basic assumptions of the strategic questioning process is that knowledge resides and is alive in all people. People see and know intimately the problems that are facing them, and they are probably in the best position to collectively design

alternatives for themselves. The point here is to ask questions in such a way that it lets the ideas and energy come from the individual or system itself rather than from the social change worker.

It's not my job to figure out in my mind what a person should do and then somehow get her to do it. I need to stay out of the way. My opinions will not serve. My opinions will not be empowering to the person being questioned, and will not be useful. The people being questioned need to figure out where they need to move. The greatest service that I can provide is simply to dynamically listen, ask good questions, rephrase and reflect what they are saying back to them, and generally help them see their own pathway through the problems.

For years we have had the image of the social change worker standing in front of the crowd and saying, "Here's what we have to do." I am not suggesting that we replace leadership, but that the leaders of the group spend a significant amount of time listening to the members, the citizens they are trying to serve, and to their "adversaries," and then distill what has been heard before strategy is determined. Ideas are synthesized from the listening work rather than coming solely from the leader's own mind or from one's own immediate circle.

We all know of many people who are perfectly content to tell you what you should do. They are people who love to dispense "solutions." And we all know of experts who go from one country to another or from one society within a country to another society, telling people what to do. I call it the "consultancy disease." A change that happens as a result of the "this is what I think you should do" school of consultancy is often shallow and too fast for it to have a long lasting effect. It is not empowering for the people who are trapped within the issues at stake. The people involved might look as if they have changed, but because the change strategy has not come from them, they don't own it, and they have not invested themselves in the change.

Most people, maybe you, have had the experience of going to a friend for advice and finding yourself saying things that surprised you. You were saying things with a wisdom you didn't know you possessed, putting ideas together in a fresh way that seemed clear, coherent, and profound. Without giving advice, the questioner-friend helped you think freshly and come up with a plan of action that felt clear and uncluttered, free of all the upset and confusion that beset you before the conversation. If advice was offered it was probably in an empowering way, "You might consider (an option) but whatever you decide I will love and respect you. I know *you* will know best what to do . . . ."

When using strategic questioning in a social change campaign, you might similarly say, "I think . . . but I surely don't see the picture through your eyes. Let us work to find an alternative that meets both of our needs. Even if we differ in our opinions, I respect you and will work with you to find the best way to deal with our common situation."

Strategic questioning does not require that the practitioner forget about his or her own opinions. That would be disrespectful to yourself! It only means that you carry your opinions in a way that does not interfere with the dialogue, the respect, and the exploration of alternatives that you are trying to achieve.

Look for the "change view" of the people affected.

Individuals and societies have discrete and hidden views of how change happens. The strategic questioner needs to find out how the major players on an issue explain the social changes they have seen. The strategies they are willing to use to create change in their lives, institutions, and communities will predominantly come from their "change view."

For instance, if you ask people in the United States to tell you what changes they have seen in their society they will give a whole list. One of their frequent observations is that people's smoking habits have changed significantly, and that smoking in public buildings has become minimal. When asked how this change came about people mention changes in the laws that prohibit smoking in certain places, the lobbying of anti-smoking groups, research showing that even passive smoking is dangerous to health, educational articles promoting quitting smoking, or lawsuits against cigarette companies. All these represent different strategies for making social change happen.

It is my experience that the people who mentioned educational campaigns are the most likely to put their money and energy into future educational campaigns concerning some other social change issue. Those mentioning lawsuits will support challenges in court or might be lawyers themselves. Writers often credit change as coming from popular articles and so forth. Understanding the change views of individuals gives us clues about the strategies that these people will support in future campaigns in their community or society.

Create a neutral common ground.

When a questioner is perceived as committed to an impartial stance, and enters into a highly charged political problem, then people on all sides of the issue are given a safe space to let off steam and explore alternatives. A team testing this theory in the early 1980s questioned many people in the Middle East about the conflicts within the region. To the PLO (the Palestine Liberation Organization) they asked, "Why doesn't the PLO recognize Israel?" To the Israelis they asked, "What is keeping Israel from creating self-rule for Palestine?" The pat answers of course came out first. Everyone knows the answers available from the strong ideologies that surround the issues of the Middle East. But with more questioning in a neutral way, we can help each of the parties think freshly in an as-yet-undiscovered place for them.

When Barbara Walters, the ABC-TV interviewer, asked Anwar Sadat, "What would it take for you to go to Jerusalem and meet with Menachem Begin?" suddenly Sadat was examining the obstacles to this goal in a new way.

Identified as a neutral party to the conflict, Barbara Walters asked a strategic question at just the right moment. She enabled Sadat to think freshly about the political realities and envision a different reality of his own making. As he talked, he found his own way to break through those obstacles and move the issues forward toward greater peace in the Middle East.

Create respect.

The strategic questioning process is a way of talking with people with whom you have differences without abandoning your own beliefs and yet looking for the common ground between you. This requires a basic sense of respect for the person being questioned. In every heart rests some ambiguity, in every ideology some parts don't fit. Your job is not to judge the responses to your questions, but to look for the potential for this person to make her or his own movement on the issue at stake.

Strategic questioning assumes that both I and my "adversary" want to do better than we are presently doing. We start by creating a basic feeling of respect between us. For example, take a developer, such as a sand miner or a timber logger. The developer's heart probably hides a certain ambivalence about what he or she is doing, and at least a part of him or her wants to be doing better for the earth, better for all its creatures.

Strategic questions assume that the common ground is "findable" by both of us in dialogue. We explore alternatives together, with respect—that is the key. Here we can discover a real commitment to pluralism of ideas and worldviews. And we learn not only how to cope with the differences between us but also how to make it work for us both institutionally and socially. Within a world being torn apart by seemingly irreconcilable differences, creating such respect is really a key task for these times.

Listen to pain.

Listening to suffering is one of the most important things a social change worker can do. The job is not only to listen but also to let the suffering fully into your heart without denying its reality. This task takes both courage and vulnerability on the part of the questioner. You may find yourself confronting your own limitations of heart, your own sense of helplessness surrounding the issues at stake. You may find yourself considering radical alternatives to this suffering as well as the many levels of meaning it may have.

When you ask questions about the important things in life you're going to touch sore spots. People are so scared, so hurt by their own powerlessness, that opening up a subject like poverty and homelessness, the threat of nuclear war, the oppression of racial and ethnic groups, a sick river, the oppression of gays and lesbians, violence, or any other politically hot topic may be overwhelming to the people being questioned.

When faced with the pain of others, it is important to give it your fullest attention, as if someone's life depended on it. Though you may be tempted here to think that the pain you may be witnessing is only an individual suffering, all individual suffering is tied to our collective suffering. And institutional and community ways exist that can address or ignore the issue that gives rise to individual pain.

Empathy is the skill of saints. It might take you a bit longer to deal with suffering. Don't expect to be in the presence of pain and not be profoundly affected by it. When we are at the edge of what we feel comfortable with, we may feel a kind of vertigo that threatens to pull us into a void and join the pain and the rage that goes with it. Will you go over the edge or stay here? Be patient with yourself and the people you are questioning. Listening is caring. Allowing change to ripen is caring. Caring is healing. By bringing strategic questions into a world of suffering, you can become part of that world learning to heal itself, looking for ways that the pain can move.

Go Forth and Question!

Strategic questioning can be a personal process if used between two people for their own growth and change, or it can be a political process when considering changes among groups and institutions working for the common good. You can practice strategic questioning through everyday conversation. I urge people to learn by practicing these processes in twos and threes, as it is often very difficult to think of long-lever questions while listening one-on-one in a conversation. Listening is challenging, thinking of long-lever questions is challenging, and living in the world is hard, so I think it is easier to learn to ask strategic questions when you can sit back a bit. You need to observe and get enough distance to examine the unexamined assumptions, look for movement, and think of the unaskable. Remember that profound change can take a long time and the slowest changes often prove to be the deepest. Also, while the process may take many years the change becomes visible from one moment to the next, seeming as if a miracle has occurred.

I have found the process of strategic questioning brings up our deeply personal visions of the future. Even subjects like sex and money pale in contrast to our deeper feelings about our dreams and fears for the health of the earth and our own society. The current political system is characterized by static and cynical thinking that only barely masks our fears and dreams about our collective lives. I do not see apathy in our citizenry; I see a deep fear of caring too much and a fear of being disappointed. I see an apathetic people who are being fed information about the world in passive and isolating ways, and who are afraid they will lose what they have if they challenge that passivity. I see a people who have fallen out of touch with the habits of liberation. I see a people longing for a way to move to a better relationship with themselves, with their families, and with their society. I also see a people who are experiencing change. And I see the shock that accompanies change, as people try to figure out the implications of these changes on their lives and institutions.

So few ways remain for us to show our caring in the world without risking being ripped off or manipulated into some ego-driven or sectarian campaign. We have learned to suspect political double-talk and group-think, which has left us unable to acknowledge our longings for real political change.

But we can act. We must accept the responsibility that whatever we do—or don't do—impacts on the ways of life we all share. We are always involved even if we are sitting on the sideline. We are consuming resources, having relationships, working toward goals. There is no way we are not involved in what is happening. The question is, How best can we be involved? We can start with deep and dynamic listening and questioning where the solutions are limited only by our imaginations. Our neighbors and coworkers have important strategical information. So do we. When we listen deep into the heart where courage and intelligence live, strategies may be liberated into action.

Stories of Strategic Questioning

Often stories facilitate understanding. Each example illustrates how strategic questioning was used in practice and illuminates many of the points made in this chapter.

Questions That Are Cleaning the Ganges

I'm from Idaho. I don't know if you know what that means, but it's very hard for a person from Idaho to think of cleaning up the Ganges River. About as far as you can get from cleaning up the Ganges River is Idaho. When a friend from India asked me to help him clean up the river, I knew I had no experience cleaning up rivers. I knew nothing about sewage. What I did know about was how to build a strategy for social change. It seemed that was what they needed.

When I first went to India I used strategic questioning. I began by building a series of questions, starting with how they saw the problem themselves. "What do you see when you look at the river?" "How do you explain the situation with the river to your children?" "How do you feel about the condition of the river?" I listened very carefully to how they explained to themselves what they saw. Essentially I was looking at their logic as well as their words. I was looking for the cultural wiring around the river.

I couldn't say, " Oh, I see the river's polluted." If I said that it would be like my saying in a Western context, "Your mother is a whore." In the context of India, it would be a cultural insult, and the Indians would stop listening. It would create reaction and resistance. So I had to find out how they explained the pollution to themselves.

Over and over again I heard something like, "The river is holy, but she is not pure. We are not taking care of her the way she needs us to." The funny thing is that, after hearing this reply, I noticed that I started to personally think less in terms of "pollution" and more in terms of "people not taking care of the river." This shift was an important change of perspective for me. Pollution is an abstraction that avoids addressing the responsibility of the people who are making the mess—by focusing the attention solely on the river. It is almost as if the river is to blame for being polluted!

Very often people also said, "I see the problem, but others don't." This answer told me a lot about the taboos of the society, and the distance between people. Such a response told me what the Indians I spoke with can and cannot talk about with each other. Often in a situation such as the holy Ganges, the symbolic overload is so great that to talk about what you really think may seem sacrilegious or crazy to others.

I needed to understand their change view—how they expected change to happen, what kind of strategies they had confidence in. In India, no social change can compare to the liberation of their country from the control of the British, and this affects their views on how change happens. When I asked how that change had happened, I heard many strategies for change—satyagraha, fasting, direct action, pressuring civic leaders, citizen's assemblies, marches to the capitol—stories of change that are embedded in that culture. These also became the strategies they were willing to use now to clean their holy river. I would then ask, "What would you like to do to clean the river?" They would then think further, taking their change view and applying it to this specific situation.

For several years the Foundation held a citizen's assembly where officials in charge of the Ganga Action Plan came to a large multicolored tent to discuss the progress of the work and plans with members of the Foundation and the local citizens. In this public forum the officials gave their presentations and then citizens stood up at the microphone and gave their own ideas and asked questions. This kind of lobbying is a strategy that goes on all the time in India. We have talked about direct actions and other strategies but the people are not yet ready for a public campaign. It is clear to me that the members of the Foundation have a very precise idea of what to do when the right time comes.

One thirteen-year-old young man suggested that he and his friends would like to "get some sticks and go up and down the river and persuade people not to toilet on the river." I did not evaluate this idea but passed it on evenhandedly to the Foundation members. They recognized the seeds of a great idea in the one the young man offered. Thus the idea of the home guard was born, and for five years or so this consisted of a team of adults who walked along the riverfront of the city, or traveled on the river in a boat. Equipped with sticks but no guns, their task was to discourage citizens from acts disrespectful to the river like toileting, washing with soap, and dumping animal carcasses into the river. Before you get too judgmental about these behaviors which may seem strange to you, you need to recognize that most people in India do not have private bathrooms in their homes, and it is hard in a city of over a million to find bare land to bury cows, goats, and dogs when they die.

People often told me how impossible it was to clean the river. Rather than assuming it was impossible, I started to think that maybe it was going to take quite a long time and I had better start thinking about the next generation in my questioning. I was already questioning young people but I added a question for the adults, "How are you preparing your children to clean up the river?"

Everyone in the Foundation was asked that question and to a person they had said something like, "We are doing nothing to prepare the children to clean the river." But now their great love of the river, their love for their children, and the void in their answers to that question could not long exist in the same minds. The dissonance was too great.

One afternoon when I was taking a shower, someone came running in and said, "Peavey, come right away, we've got a great idea." I thought, "Gosh, you know, I rarely get summoned from the shower with a great idea." So I quickly dressed and combed my hair and went to find them. They were gathered and enthusiastically discussing a plan: "We're going to have a poster-painting contest for the children. We'll have all the students in Benares draw posters about what they see regarding the health of the river. And we'll hang the winning posters up at a large musical event. The adults will see what the children see and be embarrassed . . . ."

It was an original idea and clearly the idea was theirs. Everybody in that room had been asked a question about the preparation of their children for river-cleaning work. Could that question have had anything to do with the emergence of the idea about the poster contest? I believe it did. But I surely didn't come up with that idea and since it was their idea, they had enthusiasm around it. We have had poster contests almost every year since then. Five to eight hundred young people have regularly gathered on the banks of the Ganges in poster-making competitions.

People need to come up with their own answers. Questioning can catalyze this process. A powerful question has a life of its own as it chisels away at the problem. Don't be disappointed if a great question does not have an answer right away. A very powerful question, a long-lever question, may not have an answer at the moment it is asked. It will sit rattling in the mind for days or weeks as the person works on an answer. If the seed is planted, the answer will grow. Questions are alive!

Questioning a Hydroelectric Plant
A group in Australia was concerned about a hydroelectric plant that was planned for Ravenshoe, Queensland. They found strategic questioning a powerful tool for raising the issues that concerned them. Maintaining a

nonpartisan stance also had advantages in engaging in dialogue. As Bryan Law, a member of the organizing group, writes:

"We made our first step into the public community life of Ravenshoe. . . . . We decided that step would be humble, and would consist of listening to the opinions, ideas and feelings of local people (rather than preaching our ideas to them). To do this, we constructed a survey questionnaire, which asked thirty open-ended questions about the Ravenshoe community, and the potential impact of the Tully Millstream project on that community . . . . I found two points of great interest in conducting this survey.

"First, almost everyone who approached our table wanted to know 'which side' we were on. It was almost as if public debate had decreed this as an either/or issue. Our group had agreed earlier on a response to this question, which was that while individual members had their own opinions, the group as a whole was impartial. We didn't want to take a side. We wanted to listen to all sides. It was amazing to see how people opened up after this response, and shared what they thought and felt.

"I began to see the potential for resolution of this problem. I began to ask myself (and others) the questions: (i) what kind of hydro project could we find consensus support for to build in this district? (escaping the yes/no false dichotomy) (ii) what positive and co-operative steps could we take on other issues and problems in the district?

"Second, having said we were impartial it became so. I found personally I could not repeat the formula without making it true. My mind opened up. I lost my previous certainties, and began to really listen for the first time. I found I didn't have all the answers. This was a bit uncomfortable for a while, but gradually I began to recognize it for the truly empowering process it was.

"We feel it is important . . . to encourage local residents (and everyone else) not to over-simplify the issues and continue the polarization. Instead, to recognize the range of insights, opinions, perspectives, and knowledge within the district, and to see this diversity as a potential source of strength. Conflict can generate much creativity if handled the right way. . . . The attitude of the QEC (Queensland Electric Corporation) is that they have proposed a scheme, and it is the best one possible. If it goes ahead they will begin to meet local responsibilities. If it doesn't, they won't. This attitude looks to be the biggest single impediment to a constructive resolution of conflict. . . .

"The group held a public meeting to discuss the electric plant. About 180 people came and perhaps 100 of them clapped loud and long at one man's suggestion that we get out of town. Sitting there with these feelings of apparent hatred washing over us in waves was not an experience any of us is keen to repeat.

"However, there were positive aspects of the night. Many of those other eighty people, who witnessed the attacks on us, and who had until then been suspicious or noncommittal, came down off their fence and began to send messages of active support. About thirty people stayed to help us clean up, and asked us not to give up. They said that what we had done was worthwhile. We received promises of financial and other support.

"Towards the end of the meeting, a small number of conservative people who are prominent in the community, and who strongly support the dam, were also offering constructive comments on our efforts. I think this represents one of the key dynamics of nonviolence that when people are attacked for holding principled views, and do not respond in kind but stay constructive, those doing the attacking lose support. Those holding to truth and love gain."*

Questioning and Water

Sue and Col Lennox came to one of my workshops on strategic questioning in Sydney, Australia. The following Monday morning they returned to the schools in Manley, Australia, where they teach. The students were in an uproar about a chemical spill in the creek behind their school. All the fish in the lagoon (which is fed by the creek) were dying. Sue thought, "Here is a chance to practice strategic questioning."

She taught the children briefly how to do it by asking:

"What do you see ?" "What do you know?"

"How do you feel?"

"How could it be?" " How should it be?"

"What needs to be changed?"

"What should we do?"

"What can you do?"

"What support do you need?"

The students went out to use these strategic questions to question their neighbors, their fellow students, and teachers. They also went to the creek and consulted the creek. In doing this they opened their hearts to the pain of the creek. They knew that they had to do something. They came back from their consultations with many perceptions and expressions of concern. From their questioning they had uncovered some good ideas of what to do and what others would be willing to do.

The students had to determine which ideas fit their own talents and time, and which seemed to be the best ideas. For the past three years they have been working on testing the water of that creek, talking to the local city council and community, finding the exact nature of the pollution of the creek, making videotapes, and teaching other students all over Australia to do the same. All this was catalyzed by the strategic questioning process.

---

*Excerpted from Bryan Law, "Toward Nonviolence in Ravenshoe, Part 2" *Nonviolence Today*, 25 (March/April 1992): p. 3-6.

Questioning the Media's View of Women

A couple of weeks after attending a strategic questioning workshop in Auckland, New Zealand, a woman saw a television show about violence against women. The show did not adequately condemn such violence and it carried a commercial that she thought was also anti-women. The women's community in Auckland was upset about this show and the commercial. They put out the message that women should call the manager of the station and give him a piece of their minds.

This particular woman decided to see what would happen if she tried strategic questioning. She called the manager but instead of lecturing him about what she thought, she started off with some questions: "How does a show get on the air?" "What review policies do you have about combining commercials and the content of your shows?" "How could the women's community work with the television station to create better programming around this issue?" Notice here the "how could . . ." nature of the question. If she had phrased the question, "Is there a way we could work together . . ." she might have received the answer, "No, there is no way." This success story exemplifies why you should avoid questions that set up a "yes or no" answer.

Finally the manager said, "Say, you seem to be quite knowledgeable about this matter. Would you like to be on the advisory board that screens each show and commercial and decides what should go on the air?" No others who had called with their opinion were invited into this powerful board. Her questioning opened valuable doors to cooperation and common ground.

Questioning Nuclear War

The nature of strategic questioning may well uncover upsetting feelings on the part of the person being questioned. Deborah Lubar wrote a moving account of a door-to-door listening exercise she undertook on the issue of nuclear war. Her task was to find out what people were thinking, rather than try to convince them of anything. Pad in hand she introduced herself, and asked the following questions:

> "What do you think the greatest problem facing the world is today?"
>
> "What do you consider the chances of nuclear war to be?"
>
> "What do you think would make our country safe and strong?"

While these are not particularly dynamic questions, they are open and invite deep thinking. She came to a house where a man grudgingly let her in . . . and then turned quite hostile. When she asked him about nuclear war he barked, "No, no, no, I don't have time for these ridiculous questions." She left stunned by his rudeness.

A few minutes later, she was coming out of another house. There the man stood with his arms crossed, waiting for her. "What do you expect me to do about it?" he demanded belligerently. Now she had a problem. She had opened up an issue and it was clearly difficult for him to deal with his fear and helplessness. He said, "I'm sorry I threw you out of my house, but what do you expect me to do about it? For God's sake, what do you want?" They went for a walk as he pelted her with questions. Finally, he shook her hand and walked away.

The next day, Deborah followed an impulse and went back to the man's house. She felt a bit like a fool. What excuse could she give for returning? Finally she just went to the door. The man answered, surprised but pleased to see her. He told her that he had had a horrible night, sweating through nightmares about nuclear war.

He had an emotionally sensitive button, as we all do, that is about control and change. Deborah's questions pushed that button. Immediately he felt his helplessness and his fear of how much he cared. It might sometimes look like apathy, but I think apathy is usually actually a fear of caring too much. The questions that Deborah asked pushed the button and upset emerged.

They talked of many things until the man realized he was late for work. At the door he took her hands and they looked at each other straight in the eye. Deborah later wrote, "What we learned of one another that morning was profoundly intimate and it had only to do with our common bond as two human beings groping in the dark to confront the difficult times we live in."*

There is a part of each of us that desires to keep life static. Isn't it peculiar? Don't you wonder why it is that when we're changing we're also the most alive, the most juicy, the most open. But we fear change the most. It's a puzzlement, isn't it? A real puzzlement.

---

*Adapted from a story in my book, *Heart Politics* (Philadelphia: New Society Publishers, 1986), pp. 167–168.

Appendix I

GROUP PROCESS
RESOURCES

COMMUNICATION AGREEMENT

Carolyn R. Shaffer and Kristin Anundsen*

Take responsibility for your own feelings. Do not expect others to read your mind. Use "I statements" and refrain from blaming.

Communicate directly with the person or persons involved in an issue. Do not work through go-betweens or serve as a go-between for others. If someone asks you for information about an issue in which you are not directly involved, direct him or her to the proper source.

Do not speak critically about others behind their backs unless you voice the same criticisms to their faces. To avoid unhelpful speculation, give specific names when you make a critical comment in a meeting.

State your position or concern before asking how others feel about it. Do not set someone up to give a "wrong" answer. Be courageous and put yourself on the spot first.

Practice active listening. Listen silently and with your whole self until the speaker has finished speaking. Then restate what the speaker has said and wait for confirmation.

Provide continual feedback. Do not allow resentments to build up, and do not forget to give positive strokes.

Respect and validate others' feelings. If you do not agree or do not support another's statement, acknowledge what has been said, then make your point.

Use humor softly, not sharply.

---

*Shaffer, Carolyn R., and Kristin Anundsen. *Creating Community Anywhere*. New York: Tarcher/Perigree, 1993, p. 252.

THE "TEN COMMANDMENTS" FOR GROUP CONVERSATION

*Elissa Melamud**

1. Confidentiality. What goes on in the group stays in the group. Gossip outside about others, even among group members, is discouraged.

2. Empathy. Probably the best thing you can do for someone is to listen and show you've heard. This is different from praise, blame, advice, or reassurance. Most people can solve their own problems if given receptive attention and honest feedback. This is, in fact, a good definition of support.

3. Always speak for yourself. Make "I statements." For example, say, "I think...", not "We (He, She, They, Some people) think."

4. When speaking of someone in the group, always speak directly to him or her. Instead of, "John over there..." say, "You, John...."

5. Don't turn statements into questions. Questions are often disguised statements. Make statements outright. For example, instead of "Who cares?" you might say, "I feel that no one cares." Also, questions shift the emphasis from yourself to another person. Keep the emphasis on yourself.

6. Do not use statements that are cop-outs. If you examine your everyday speech patterns, you may discover some phrases that you use to avoid seeing or expressing your own feelings. Here are some common examples: "I don't know" (really means: "I don't want to know"). "Don't ask me" (really means: "You'll be mad if I tell you"). "I can't" (really means "I don't want to"). "That's the way it is" (really means: "I won't do anything about it").

7. Speak in the present tense. Feelings are sometimes lost by being expressed in the past tense. Do not say, "I thought" or "I felt" but rather, "I think" or "I feel." This will make you more aware of your own feelings and better able to communicate them to others.

8. Share, but don't force feelings or personal disclosure. People should not feel pressured to share their personal histories, but as feelings come up, it's good to share them as openly as possible.

9. Don't force participation. Each person has the right to "pass" on a given activity.

10. Take responsibility for your own reactions and avoid the victim role. Example: "I feel belittled by what you just said" takes responsibility. "You really put me down!" does not. In general, "I statements" enhance taking of responsibility.

---

*From "Peace Circles."

GIVING EFFECTIVE FEEDBACK

Peter Woodrow

We all need to learn to give feedback to people so that they can hear it, absorb it, and evaluate it for themselves—and then change behavior which affects their relationships with others. Most of us have trouble telling other people what we think or feel about things they do that bother us or which affect groups we are a part of. We all remember times when someone told us something about ourselves and it felt awful—and we don't want to inflict that kind of pain on anyone else. However, by avoiding telling people what they need to hear (and we need to say!), we abort what can be a creative process of growing and changing together.

Most people really do want to hear what other people have to say about them, both positive and negative. We all look for signals and messages from our families, friends, colleagues, co-workers, clients, and acquaintances. When someone takes the time to think about us and give direct information about how we are perceived, it can be an affirming experience. Some specific suggestions:

Ask "permission" to give feedback.

People hear and accept information better when they have asked for it affirmatively. At times, as parents, teachers, or supervisors, we are expected to give feedback. But, even in those cases, you will be more likely to be heard if the person welcomes what you have to say.

> *"George, I would like to talk with you about your interaction with the group in the meeting this morning. Would you be interested in hearing my perceptions?"*

Provide descriptive not evaluative information.

Describe how you were affected by the actions or words of the person, allowing him or her to decide whether it was helpful or destructive—partly depending on his or her intent.

> *"Ginny, a few minutes ago you criticized my idea without acknowledging any positive aspects or giving respect for my thinking. I found that hurtful."*

Give specific and behavioral feedback, not general characterizations.

Avoid judgments such as "you are rude and uncaring" or "you are a manipulating powermonger." These don't communicate as effectively as statements of specific incidents and behaviors which caused you problems.

> "Ron, in our meeting today, I noticed that you interrupted women in the group each time they spoke and mostly dismissed their ideas. You didn't even let Joan finish describing her proposal before you cut her off with a third repeat of your own suggestion. That made me very uncomfortable and angry with you."

Take account of timing and the needs of both the giver and receiver of feedback.

Find a time to provide feedback when you as giver are feeling relatively relaxed—i.e., not when you have just been told to cut your budget by 30 percent or that your best worker is quitting. Also consider the timing from the receiver's point of view, the stress points for him or her. Try to time feedback as close to the behaviors involved as possible.

Check whether they have received the message.

Ask the person to paraphrase his or her understanding of what you have tried to communicate. In this way, you can tell if the message has gotten through—and then restate and clarify as needed.

> "OK, I've been describing the situation as I see it. I'd like to hear you tell me in your own words what you think I have been trying to say."

Other Points

Direct feedback towards behavior that the person can actually do something about.

Avoid criticising people for *who they are*—young or old, women or men, black or white, boring or ebullient. Rather, address specific behaviors which they can change if they choose to.

Own your own feelings.

Not "some people think..." or "some people in the group are saying...." Rather: "When you do _____, I feel_____, because_____."

Affirm the person when sincerely possible, but avoid the "one-two punch."

Not: "You're a really nice guy and I like you a lot, but you are making a mess of our staff meetings." Rather: "I appreciate your active participation and the many ideas you offer to the group. I think that people could hear your ideas better if you change the way you interact with people. Let me be specific...."

Making positive affirmation a regular and frequent part of your interaction with people makes it easier to give negative feedback when you need to.

Acknowledge your part of the problem, when relevant.

State feelings or actions of yours which contribute to the problem. "I know that I have not laid out clear expectations about prompt arrival at work, which may have added to the issue of your latenesses."

Practice ahead of time.

If you are uncomfortable or nervous, then find someone who can listen confidentially to you, to check your perceptions, motivations, and clarity. If you are anxious about giving feedback, try roleplaying it a few times.

Get third-party assistance.

In some circumstances, you may want to ask a third person to join you, someone who is acceptable to you and the other person. This person can act as a communications facilitator, making sure you are both hearing each other and providing safety—but definitely not trying to solve the problem.

Be prepared to listen to feedback directed at you from someone to whom you have given feedback!

QUAKER RESOURCES ON CLEARNESS AND SPIRITUAL DISCERNMENT

A BRIEF HISTORY OF CLEARNESS AMONG QUAKERS AND OTHERS

Peter Woodrow

The use of clearness committees, and related processes, has a long history within the Society of Friends (Quakers), beginning during the first decades of its existence in the last half of the 17th century.

Quakerism is a mystical spiritual movement, believing that each individual has the capacity to develop a personal relationship with God within and to be guided by that Inner Teacher. A person living true to that "Light Within" or "Inner Teacher," then, might be "led" to some action or ministry. Quakers were often persecuted for actions in obedience to such inwardly revealed truth. For example, Quakers held strongly to the equality of persons and refused to give "hat honor" (taking off one's hat to a superior) which led frequently to arrest, fines and imprisonment. In the early days of the Quaker movement, some claimed leadings took idiosyncratic—and sometimes bizarre—forms, such as walking naked through the streets. Some of these actions led to unnecessary persecution and controversy among Quaker groups.

There arose, then, a need to subject the spiritual leadings sensed by one member of the religious community to group or corporate "testing," as a way to protect against scattered and individualistic actions. After all, Quakers asserted (and still assert) that there is one Truth to which we can each bear witness. If we receive contradictory messages regarding the Truth, someone, or all, must be in error. The only solution in this case is to wait upon further guidance from God moving among the faithful.

As the Society of Friends became more organized, it usually fell to the elders of the meeting (the Quaker equivalent of the local church) to perform the function of testing spiritual leadings encountered by members. In practice, a member of the meeting who felt the welling up of a concern or the call to travel and preach to a certain people brought that concern or call before the elders. The group listened to the message and "held it in the Light"—that is, they worshipped together to seek clarity corporately about the authenticity of the leading. In a sense, they acted as a clearness group, deciding, together with the individual who heard the call, whether the leading arose out of the Spirit or from other voices of self-aggrandizement, ego-fulfillment, need for attention, and so on.

In some cases, Friends who felt leadings were confused by them or resistant to doing what seemed to be asked of them. Some of them went to the elders to share the religious insight they had received, but expressing a wish not to carry it out. In at least some instances, the elders in worship decided that the Friend in question had better follow the leading, even though there was no evident logic to the proposed action at the time. Faithfulness to the leading had unexpected results at times. In other instances, elders questioned the source or authenticity of the call and counseled against action or for further waiting or "seasoning" of the concern.

Eighteenth-century Quaker John Woolman heard many leadings to carry a call to Quakers to give up the practice of holding slaves, and became a pioneer in the early antislavery movement. In many instances, he met with elders from his own meeting or from elsewhere to consider his response to the leadings and how he might carry them out. Throughout the eighteenth and nineteenth century, hundreds of Friends experienced leadings which they brought to the elders for clearness: to travel in the ministry, to establish a new school, to provide aid to Native American groups, to work for women's suffrage or against slavery.

In modern days, clearness has been used most frequently among Quakers as a process for a local Friends Meeting to approve marriage or to accept new members. A couple desiring to be married "under the care of the meeting" writes the meeting declaring their wish. The meeting appoints a clearness committee which meets with the couple to determine if they are, in fact, "clear for marriage." In most cases, particularly in the past, the group was trying to make sure that the couple was clear from other entanglements or obligations. Nowadays the committee is more likely to probe to see if the couple is truly ready for the commitment entailed in marriage, and to consider whether the marriage is appropriately performed under the care of the meeting. If the committee decides that the couple is clear, they report back to the monthly meeting which then proceeds with arrangements for the marriage.

Similarly, a person who would like to join a meeting writes a letter to the meeting and states this intention. The meeting, in response, appoints a clearness committee (which sometimes has other names) to meet with the prospective member to see if the person is "clear for membership." In some cases, the committee and the prospective member might discover that the person is not ready—because they do not fully understand Friends practices or because they have doubts due to lingering attachment to another faith tradition. If the person and the committee find the person clear, they report back the meeting as a whole, which accepts the new member.

Note that in the cases of marriage and membership, the appointed clearness committee is charged with the task of actually making a decision, because they must bring a recommendation back to the monthly meeting, so that the meeting itself can take action (take the marriage under its care or accept a person into membership). In the broader application of clearness, normally the meeting is not asked to take action and the ultimate decision is entirely up to the person initiating the clearness process.

Since the late 1960s, some Friends meetings have begun to use clearness in broader ways, as a resource in the meeting community for Friends who sense a calling or "leading," who are at the point of an important decision in family or career, or who are in crisis and need help through a specific set of decisions.

The history of this revival of clearness among Friends is a bit murky. However, it appears that it was initiated in the 1960s by young Friends active in Young Friends of North America. Several of these Young Friends were immersed in the history and practices of early Friends and sought to revitalize Friends' practice. A number of Young Friends participated in New Swarthmoor, an experiment in Quaker simple living and community which lasted several years (approximately 1969-1973). Within New Swarthmoor, members of the group brought matters of personal decision to the larger group and clearness committees were formed to assist in the individual's decision process.

Some young Quakers who had been active in Young Friends of North America and/or New Swarthmoor also became engaged in Movement for a New Society (MNS), a nation-wide and international network of nonviolent social change groups which was founded in 1971. One of the antecedent groups of MNS was A Quaker Action Group. However, at its founding, MNS decided that it would not (could not) be a Quaker group, since its ambitious program of social transformation required participation by people from diverse backgrounds. Nevertheless, many Quakers were involved, and MNS borrowed freely from many Quaker practices, including a secular form of consensus decision making and the use of clearness for important decisions.

People became members of MNS by joining a working group or collective, and clearness was used for that decision process. In MNS living communities, members joined cooperative households through a modified clearness process as well. As MNS members came upon important decision points in their personal and political lives, clearness was employed as a way for the community to assist the decision of the individual. Based on that experience, a clearness manual, *Clearness: Processes for Supporting Groups and Individuals in Decision-Making* (1976), was written (Section II of this book is a revised version of that manual).

Over time, the experiments with clearness, both from Young Friends and from the applications within MNS, began to seep back into the practice of Friends meetings. The *Clearness* manual, even though written for social change groups, was adapted for use by many Friends meetings. By the middle of the 1980s materials on clearness written specifically for use by Friends began to appear, some of which are reproduced in this appendix. Others are listed in the bibliography.

The basic concept of engaging the religious community in the process of individual spiritual discernment has also begun to gain interest in non-Quaker groups. Several Catholic orders now use clearness-like processes to aid personal discernment. And some other Protestant churches have developed discernment procedures similar to clearness within their community life. (See *Listening Hearts: Discerning Call in Community*, listed in the bibliography.)

Clearness is a flexible concept which will continue to develop among Friends and others who seek to bridge the gap between personal and private matters and the caring spiritual and/or activist community of support.

CLEARNESS COMMITTEES AND THEIR USE IN PERSONAL DISCERNMENT

*by Jan Hoffman**

A clearness committee meets with a person who is unclear on how to proceed in a keenly felt concern or dilemma, hoping that it can help this person to reach clarity. It assumes that each of us has an Inner Teacher who can guide us, and, therefore, that the answers sought are within the person seeking clearness. It also assumes that a group of caring friends can serve as channels of divine guidance in drawing out that Inner Teacher.

The purpose of the committee members is not to criticize or to offer their collective wisdom; they are to listen without prejudice or judgment, to help clarify alternatives, to help communication if necessary, and to provide emotional support as an individual seeks to find "truth and the right course of action." The committee must remember that people are capable of growth and change. They must not become absorbed with historical excuses or reasons for present problems, but rather focus on what is happening now and explore what could be done to resolve it.

In a monthly meeting, persons may ask Ministry and Counsel (Worship and Ministry or Overseers) to form a clearness committee. The focus person may also choose her or his committee, gathering five or six trusted friends with as much diversity among them as possible. In either case, formation should be under a discipline of worship, taking care that people are chosen not just because they are friends, but through some discernment process. Note that the process is always initiated by the person seeking clearness, though a friend may ask, "Would a clearness committee be helpful?"

A clerk and recorder should be appointed. The clerk opens the meeting, closes it, and serves as traffic cop in between, making sure that the rules are followed, that everyone who wants to speak may do so, and that there is a common understanding of the degree of confidentiality about the meeting. The clerk also sees to physical details which will nurture an atmosphere of seeking silence: seeing that everyone has a comfortable chair, taking any

---

*These notes are compiled by Jan Hoffman from her experience and the following sources: Parker Palmer at a conference on Solitude and Community; *Faith and Practice* of Pacific Yearly Meeting (1985), pp. 58–60; and *Living with Oneself and Others* of New England Yearly Meeting Committee on Ministry and Counsel (1985), pp. 50–55. This article may be freely reproduced with credits.

telephones off the hook, and making sure the space is enclosed and a 'do not disturb' sign is up if interruptions are likely. The recorder writes down the questions asked and perhaps some of the responses and gives this record to the focus person after the meeting.

The person seeking clearness should write up his or her question in advance of the meeting and make it available to committee members. The concern should be identified as precisely as possible: relevant background factors should be mentioned; and clues, if any, about what lies ahead should be offered. This exercise is valuable not only for the committee members, but especially for the focus person. When the committee meets, it should be for two to three hours, with the understanding that there may be a second, and even a third, meeting.

Normally, a meeting begins with a period of centering silence. When the focus person is ready, she or he begins with a brief summary of the question or concern. The rule for committee members is very simple—but very difficult to follow: members may not speak in any way except to ask the focus person a question, an honest question. That means no presenting solutions, no advice, no "Why don't you...?", no "My uncle had the same problem and he...", no "I know a good diet that would help you a lot." Nothing is allowed except honest, probing, caring, challenging, open, unloaded questions! And it is crucial that these questions be asked, not for the sake of the questioner's curiosity, but for the sake of the focus person's clarity. Caring, not curiosity, is the rule for questioners. Remember that your task is to serve as a channel for the Light to help the focus person deal with the problem or make a decision; neither you nor the committee deals directly with the problem or makes the decision.

Committee members should try to ask questions briefly and to the point, rather than larding them with a lot of background and qualifications. Not only does this help guard against turning questions into speeches, but it may also help open the focus person to some insight that gets obscured when the questions wander. Committee members should also trust their intuitions. Even if a question seems off the wall, if it feels insistent, ask it.

The focus person normally answers the questions in front of the group—and the answers generate more questions. But, it is always the focus person's absolute right not to answer—either because she or he does not know the answer, or because the answer is too personal or painful to be revealed in the group. The more often a focus person can answer aloud, the more she or he and the committee have to go on. But this should never be done at the expense of the focus person's privacy or need to protect vulnerable feelings. When answering, the focus person would do well to keep his or her responses relatively brief so time remains for more and more questions. Some questions seem to require one's whole life story in response: resist the temptation to tell it!

Do not be afraid of silence in the group. In fact, value it, treasure it. The pacing of questioning and answering should be gentle, relaxed, humane. A machine gun pace of questioning or answering destroys reflectiveness. If there is silence in the group, it does not mean nothing is happening. It may very well mean the most important thing of all is happening, inside of people.

Well before the end of the session, following at least an hour of questioning, the clerk should ask for a pause and ask the focus person how she or he wishes to proceed. This is an opportunity for the focus person to choose a mode of seeking clarity other than the questions, which have characterized the rest of the session. The recorder continues to record during this time. Possibilities are:

> Silence, out of which anyone can speak, under the same discipline as that in other meetings for worship;
>
> Silence, out of which people share images which come to them as they focus on the focus person (this process is often helped if everyone is physically touching the focus person);
>
> The committee continues with more questions;
>
> The focus person asks questions of the committee;
>
> The committee is asked to give advice;
>
> The committee is asked to affirm the gifts they see in the focus person.

Before the session ends, any clarity reached can be shared, if the focus person wishes to do so. She or he and the committee should agree on next steps. If another meeting seems right, it should be scheduled at this time. It may be that the focus person will reach clarity and no further meeting action is necessary. Or it may be clear that a support committee or an oversight committee should be appointed to aid the person in keeping clear and/or in being accountable to his or her initial clarity. Members of the clearness committee are free to release themselves from further commitment or to offer to serve.

The clearness committee works best when everyone approaches it in a prayerful mood (which does not exclude playful!), inwardly affirming the reality of each person's inner guidance and truth. We must give up the notion that we can know what another's truth is and simply try, through our own human experience, to ask questions that may help remove anything that obscures the other's inner light.

CLEARNESS AND COMMITTEES ON CLEARNESS

*Pacific Yearly Meeting**

One of the special joys of a Friends Meeting is the recurring reminder that each person contributes to the spiritual strength of the loving community and that the community is a guiding and sustaining force in the life of each individual. This mutual relationship strengthens the Meeting and produces a bond of love and trust among its members, helping the Meeting to find unity in its spiritual life and harmony in its actions. An important evidence of such spiritual unity in a meeting is that members feel free to ask for help in clarifying personal problems and in making decisions. These may relate to such matters as family adjustments, marriage difficulties, separation, divorce, stands to be taken on public issues, a new job, a required move to a distant area, a concern for personal witness, traveling in the ministry, and other personal decisions. Meetings usually respond to such requests for help by appointing committees on clearness+ (sometimes called committees of concern).

A committee on clearness meets with the seeker, not as professional counselors nor as friends discussing a problem and giving advice, but rather as caring Friends, drawing on the same resources that bind us together in meeting for worship. Maintaining a spirit of openness and prayerful waiting, the committee members seek to help the individual become clear about a problem or impending decision by serving as channels for divine guidance. Their purpose is not to criticize, to elder, nor to offer their collective wisdom; they are there to listen without prejudice or judgment, to help clarify alternatives, to help communication if necessary, and to provide emotional support, as an individual, or a small group such as a family, seeks to find God's will. As in a

---

*From *Faith and Practice* (1985), which provides guidance to Monthly Meetings, the Quaker equivalent of a congregation, which have a monthly meeting for business. Pacific Yearly Meeting is a grouping of monthly meetings in California, Nevada, Hawaii, Mexico City, and Guatemala City.

+The term "clearness" referred originally to clearness before marriage from other entangling engagements or obligations. Today, if the problem or decision involves a possible Meeting action (such as marriage, membership, release of a member, or the like), then both the Meeting and the seeker must arrive at clearness before the action may be taken.

meeting for business, all parties seek clearness, hoping to find "truth and the right course of action." In meetings of a committee on clearness, however, there is no need to find unity; the seeker's clearness is being served and the committee must finally stand aside, trusting that it may have been used to help the seeker see a problem more clearly or to make his or her own decision in the Light. In no case does a committee on clearness make the decision.

A committee on clearness is always formed at the request of the person or persons seeking clearness, though such a request may follow upon an offer by Friends in the Meeting to be of help. The seeker may initiate the forming of a committee by making a request of the Meeting, or by asking any overseer of the Monthly Meeting. In every case, the request becomes the responsibility of the Committee on Oversight.

It is the duty of the Overseers to have preliminary talks with the seeker on the nature of the problem. Such talks may convince the committee that the seeker needs professional counseling, rather than the help of a Meeting committee, and will advise the seeker accordingly. Alternatively, it may be clear to the committee that the seeker is already clear as to the course of action to be taken, but needs counsel from appropriate Friends on how to carry out the action or decision (the *how* rather than the *whether*). In such a case, the Committee on Oversight should itself counsel with the seeker.

If, however, in the judgment of the Committee on Oversight, a clearness committee is appropriate, it will, in consultation with the seeker, appoint such a committee, designating a convener from among its members. A clearness committee should be composed of persons who, because of gifts and background, seem particularly suitable to help with the problem. It is essential that a committee on clearness include only people who are acceptable both to the Committee on Oversight and to the seeker. A committee on clearness may include people of varied ages and experience, and will normally include from three to five members unless the Committee on Oversight feels that special circumstances require a larger committee.

When the problem is one in which, in the judgment of the Oversight Committee, the Meeting is too emotionally involved to be helpful, members of the committee on clearness may be selected from outside the Meeting community, from, for example, the Committee on Ministry and Oversight of the Quarterly or Yearly Meeting. It is worth repeating that Friends seek clearness in the Light; partisanship and emotional involvement are to be avoided in favor of openness and a desire to be used as a channel for the Light so that the person or persons seeking help may reach clearness.

The experience of Friends has shown the usefulness of questions like the following to be considered by persons who have been asked to serve on a committee on clearness, and of a few advices for those who agreed to do so.

Questions for Those Asked to Serve on a Committee on Clearness

1. Do you feel sufficiently at ease with the seeker and with the other members of the committee to work with them? Can you labor with them truly to provide an atmosphere in which divine guidance can be sought?

2. If it is a family decision, can you listen without prejudice or bias to each member who is involved?

3. Can you devote sufficient time and energy to this committee, knowing that it may take several meetings and many weeks or months to clarify the problem and provide support while the decision is made and carried out?

4. Can you keep the committee discussions confidential and avoid gossiping or referring to them outside the committee unless those requesting the help of the committee are comfortable with a wider sharing of their problem?

Advices for Members of a Clearness Committee

1. Try to listen to the other persons present, rather than just waiting for your turn to talk. Give equal attention to each person present, whether adult or child.

2. Remember that people are capable of change and growth. Do not become absorbed with historical excuses or reasons for present problems. Focus on what is happening now to perpetuate the situation or to require a decision.

3. Do not take sides if it is a family problem. Each person contributes to the problem, its continuation and its solution.

4. Try to avoid all suggestions of blame. It destroys openness and makes clearness difficult or impossible to reach.

5. Do not give advice; do not present solutions to others. Do not create dependency by taking over responsibility. Remember that your task is to serve as a channel for the Light to help the seeker deal with the problem or make a decision; neither you nor the committee deals directly with the problem or makes the decision.

Finally, it is important that all members of a committee on clearness feel responsibility to help the convener establish and maintain a right spirit in all meetings of the committee. The convener has the responsibility, but all members should cooperate in surrounding each meeting with a waiting silence, in beginning and ending with worship, in asking for moments of worship during a meeting, and in calling frequently to mind that a meeting of a committee on clearness is not an occasion for professional or amateur counseling, but a spiritual exercise, one in which Friends hope to be channels by means of which one or more seeking individuals may receive light on a problem and divine guidance for a decision which they—with God alone—must make.

CLEARNESS COMMITTEES, COMMITTEES OF CARE, AND OVERSIGHT COMMITTEES

Canadian Yearly Meeting*

Introduction

Faced with difficult decisions, or imperative concerns, Friends have often asked others to help discern the will of God and the leading of the Spirit in their lives. Friends in difficult situations have also asked others for help and encouragement to enable them to carry out their tasks rightly. Sometimes these arrangements are informal, sometimes the Meeting itself takes the initiative. Friends are then found who will meet those in need and offer their presence, prayers, love and support.

There are three types of committees on which Friends may draw. These are: Clearness Committees, Committees of Care, and Oversight Committees. In the work of all of these committees, the qualities of clearness and discernment are paramount.

Historically, Friends came to Meeting for help in discerning whether their concerns were spiritually based leadings, or based on their own will. The following paragraphs stem from such a background. They are relevant to the work of today's committees, which often must struggle through the more profane world of day-to-day life, and its personal problems, which Friends still seek to illumine with a spark of the divine.

Douglas Steere writes that,

> ". . . Concerns and the process of discernment require further scrutiny to understand their central place in Quaker practice. The Book of Acts in the New Testament sparkles with vivid concerns and the following of divine guidance, at no matter what the cost. Believing that we are still in the Apostolic age and that we do not work alone, Quakers have experienced in their corporate meetings for worship and their private devotions, leadings to which they have sought to be attentive. The small inner nudges . . . may be swiftly cared for, but concerns that may involve changes of career or that involve others in their unfolding call for more deliberate care. How such guidance is to be regarded and how it is to be followed raises

---

* From *Organization & Procedure* (1990)

134

the whole question of discernment. In what ways may individual Friends be helped to test the authenticity of a concern and how may they be assisted in what this may demand of them? Here again the strong corporate side of Quakerism . . . has been able to furnish spiritual assistance. . . . The traditional procedure is to call together a small committee of clearness."*

Discernment and Clearness

Some individuals are blessed with a gift for discernment—they seem to know what to do. Others must come by this skill with more effort. The key to this in the religious area is prayer. In doing this we bring ourselves into the Light. We also bring our understandings and our confusions; we bring our hopes and fears, our ambitions and desires. With divine help we may lay them all down, and be left with clarity and thanksgiving. Getting from here to there requires testing our thoughts and our feelings by the Light. We may be granted a vision of clarity directly; but more often we must look for examples of discernment reflected in the lives and decisions of others. The Bible, being a record of the work of the Spirit through history, is a most valuable source for such vicarious experiences. Friends may also make use of the Journals kept by the great ministers of our Society—George Fox, John Woolman, Elizabeth Fry, Stephen Grellet, Elias Hicks, et al.

We may also look to more recent records and the experience of those we know, and should not neglect our own journals. It is all too easy to forget an experience of divine guidance that we may have been blessed with in the past, when we are overwhelmed with a dilemma in the present. The practice of thanksgiving helps to banish forgetfulness and allows us to grow throughout our lives. Prayer and study usefully undergird the work of committees as well as individuals if they are to discern the "way forward." Where individuals feel too inexperienced to feel that they can rightly discern God's will alone in prayer, they may consult more experienced Friends—not to make their decision for them, but to help them with the process of discerning it. The most commonly used consultative process, and often the best, is for the perplexed individual to go to a number of people informally and hear what they have to say on the matter—to personal friends, colleagues, professionals and members of the Meeting, and then to meditate over what they have learned, and then act as the "way opens."

Clearness is a deep inner certainty based on spiritual discernment. Clearness takes time. It cannot be achieved for a Meeting or an individual while there is an impediment or stop in the mind. Friends' testimony is that

---

*Steere, Douglas. *Introduction to Quaker Spirituality.* Mahwah, N.J.: Paulist Press, 1984, pp. 42–43.

with divine assistance and others' help, the liberation and assurance of true clearness will come.

General Guidelines for All Three Committees

Initiation

These committees are "under the care" of Monthly, Half-Yearly, or Yearly Meetings, or their Meetings of Ministry and Counsel. Their initiation, however, differs.

> Clearness Committees are initiated by the individual, who approaches the relevant Meeting with a concern/problem that necessitates a decision. When the decision is reached, the work of the Committee ceases.

> Committees of Oversight are initiated by Meetings, which feel that the "right ordering" in carrying out something must be safeguarded.

> Committees of Care may be initiated by either the individual or the Meeting to give continuing support to the person in an undertaking, or because the person needs help.

The latter two kinds of Committees last much longer than a Clearness Committee.

Function

Committees of Care and Clearness Committees are concerned primarily with people. Committees of Oversight are concerned primarily with tasks. Thus, those Friends serving Meetings may have an Oversight Committee to which they are accountable and a Committee of Care which supports them personally.

Maintaining Function

Committees should not change their functions without reference to the authorizing body. For example, Committees of Clearness should not allow themselves to become ongoing Committees of Care, and Oversight Committees should not allow themselves to become Committees of Care while still functioning as Oversight Committees.

Membership

A membership of two to four persons is recommended. In the case of Clearness Committees and Committees of Care, the person concerned is consulted about the choice of members. In the case of Committees of Oversight, the person is not consulted.

Service on these committees can be very demanding and Meetings should be mindful that they cannot always supply the right members for such committees. If that is so, they should be prepared to reach out to other Meetings, or refer to appropriate resources in the community.

It is essential that members work as a team and do not work as individuals with the Friend concerned, without the knowledge and approval of the other members.

Clerk

The first choice for Clerk would be a Committee member who is also a member of the Meeting's Ministry and Counsel. The Clerk must see that all members are clear as to their duties, their terms of reference, and the length of service expected of them. The Clerk should oversee the sharing of expectations of one another on the part of all participants, including the Friend(s) asking assistance.

The Clerk either is, or appoints a recorder. It is the Clerk's responsibility to see that any notes are disposed of properly, according to the type of Committee. This is particularly important because documents may, on occasion, be subpoenaed by a court of law. The Clerk should consult with the Friend concerned as to how the Committee can best work with the Friend. For example, does the Friend function best in a structured, or, an informal, situation?

Resources

Committee members will find it useful to know of helpful agencies and support services, groups and individuals outside the Meeting community.

Time given to reading and prayerful preparation in advance will help to generate an atmosphere of trust and care. Only rarely will a committee have only one meeting. A reasonable interval between meetings allows for reflection, prayer, and growth for all concerned.

Meetings Conducted "In the Manner of Friends"

The location of meetings is important; there needs to be an atmosphere of privacy, comfort, and concern for the reputation of others. In all cases, the committees will maintain careful sensitivity to the privacy of the Friend(s) concerned.

In an atmosphere of support and caring, the person(s) will be free to say what they think and feel. To listen creatively involves faith in Friends' patience, a desire to understand, and help to clarify problems and needs. During meetings, the committee will raise questions, suggest options, and share experiences where appropriate. Time should be allowed for prayer.

An immediate solution is not always possible in the situations which come before us, and the seeking for divine guidance may bear fruit much later in the lives of all concerned. These committees are one way of providing friendship and assistance within the Meeting family. In all exchanges based on love we are both givers and receivers of divine blessings. The use/operation of these committees not only helps the Friends involved, but greatly strengthens the Meetings as a whole.

Notes

The recorder may make notes of the discussion and decisions. These confidential notes should be read back and copies given to the concerned Friend(s) and the Clerk of the committee. Because notes could be evidence in a court of law, when the committee is laid down, all notes and minutes should be handed over to the concerned Friend(s), to be kept or destroyed as desired. No copies should be retained by the Meeting. The committees should report to the Meeting that it has met, and, if appropriate, its decisions.

Special Guidelines for Each of the Three Committees

Clearness Committees

Purpose and Function: a) to help Friend(s) determine the will of God as well as of himself or herself in making a difficult decision; b) to help Friend(s) test the genuineness and ramifications of a concern that involves the Meeting.

The Friends with whom they consult will not make their decision for them, but will help them in the process of discerning God's will. Clearness Committees are set up for a limited time only, until the purpose is completed. They report to their appointing Meeting the dates of their meetings, and when their task is completed, so that the committee can be laid down.

Appointment: Suitability of committee members should be considered with care by the Meeting concerned, as often sensitive issues are being considered. The acceptability of suggested members should first be cleared with the Friend(s) concerned, before final appointment.

Committees of Care

Purpose and Function: a) to provide help, both practical and spiritual, during times of stress in the lives of members of the Meeting, e.g., bereavement, separation, illness, career changes, etc.; b) to sustain Friend(s) engaged in demanding Meeting work over a long period. Care must be taken not to create a dependency, but to enable Friends to be independent, and to make their own choices.

Appointment: A wider choice of people is needed for Committees of Care than for Clearness Committees, as the life of the Committee is so much longer, and the people may need to rotate. The choice of members should be approved by the Friend(s) in need. The need for the Committee should be reviewed periodically by the appointing Meeting, and the Committee should be laid down when its job is done.

Oversight Committees

Purpose and Function: An Oversight Committee is accountable to its appointing Meeting for the execution of the responsibilities of the Friend being overseen; the oversight is of the proper fulfillment of the task, and not of the person concerned. Care for the person, if necessary, is the responsibility of a Committee of Care. Membership in the two, if needed, should not overlap.

The Oversight Committee and the designated Friend(s) should meet with the Clerk of the appointing Meeting to clarify expectations, including terms of reference, responsibilities, and a clear job description, at the outset. The terms of reference should be reviewed periodically, as well as the need for the program, task, or office itself.

It is essential that an Oversight Committee function as a whole, and that its members not work independently. The Oversight Committee serves the Meeting as a two-way channel for the messages and comments on the program, task, or office being supervised. This procedure avoids the creation of tensions in the Meeting. Otherwise, a hardworking Friend serves too many masters.

Appointment: The person overseen need not be consulted on membership of the Committee. The members should have skills appropriate to what is overseen. Membership may be changed periodically by the appointing Meeting, because this committee's duration tends to be long.

SPIRITUAL DISCERNMENT: THE PERSONAL DIMENSION

*Jan Wood**

For me, all the purposes and acts of God rise from and are encompassed by God's love for humankind. The God of Judeo-Christian faith has consistently communicated, "I love you, I want to be with you." This is the theme in the narrative of the patriarchs, in the hoped-for theocracy of Israel, in the blazing anger of destruction and exile, in the provision of a remnant, in the incarnation, in the atonement, in Pentecost, and in the Kingdom-come–now and forever. "I want to eat with you, think with you, play with you, work with you, intercourse with you, share life in all of its complications and wonders." "Fear not, I am with you," has been the one promise that winds its way from Genesis through Revelation, and continues to be a witness to our hearts this very day. It is no fluke that the incarnation of Godness in human form would be called Emmanuel: God with us. The mind-boggling truth is that the *I AM*, the *ALL in ALL*, the transcendent Essence of Being, the source of all that is created wants—even yearns—to be with us. That One has made every provision to bridge the gaps between the infinite and the finite; between perfection and brokenness; between Love and alienation; between Life and Death.

The I AM did not set up moralistic hurdles for men and women to jump over to prove their Godward intentions. The Godhead did not scheme a system by which humans could earn a place in the heavens. God asked for relationship. Right and wrong. Good and bad. These are not the essential elements of our navigation towards God. The essential elements of our seeking and remaining in the Presence of God are being in the Truth of ourselves and being in the Truth of the Godhead. There is no system. It is only a relationship. As the Abraham narrative communicates, righteousness is not a matter of doing everything "right." It is a matter of being in appropriate response/position/stance with God. And thus we read in Genesis 15:6, "And he [Abraham] believed in the Lord; and He [God] reckoned it to him as righteousness." Believing was not necessarily an appropriate response to the data that Abraham would be the father of multitudes of descendants. Believing was an appropriate response in the light of *who* was giving the data.

---

*Adapted from a talk given at Friends Consultation on Discernment, Quaker Hill Conference Center, 1985. (Original document out of print.)

What is appropriate for relationship with a God of Love is to participate/to splash/to swim/to be immersed in the Essence and Presence of God. To align our very being and all that flows from it with Life in God. From this amazing and incredible union of God and human come the fulfillment of our paradoxical desires: to be totally, uniquely fulfilled in our individuality and, at the same time, to be in union with all the universe. Personhood. Fully unique. Fully joined. We are virtually driven by our natures to find this our resting place in the universe. Our home. Life.

The fact is that we humans try to find Life where it cannot be found. Life is found in total union with the Godhead. Yet, what we try to enact with Him/Her is a loose affiliation. But that does not work to bring us the deep desires of our heart. We try to eat the fruit that would lure us with godlike control and knowledge. But it doesn't work. We take shortcuts of self-absorption that leave us with ashes in our mouths. For everything that is inappropriate to the Truth of God and of ourselves is dysfunctional for Life. A distortion. A cruel counterfeit that saps our personage, our energy and leaves us with only the bitter dregs of death—now and forever. That is the essence of evil. Non-God. Non-Reality. Non-functional. Non-Life. It is the antithesis of Life, Substance, Reality. Its power is a manipulation of life's elements. It can only usurp creation and unravel it. It can never create. Its forgeries create illusion and deception. It is as solid as shadows. Yet it is no clumsy counterfeit. Even the elect can be fooled. Discernment is the Life-saving magnetism to the heart of God that reveals the forgery for what it is.

One does not escape evil by doing good behaviors. Goodness is simply a fragrance that is given off by Life, an evaporation from the essence of God. (Mark 9:18) Badness doesn't damn a person. Badness is the stench of non-alignment with Life. It is the rot, decay of that which is separated from the vitality/the sap of aliveness.

Therefore, to discuss the problem of discernment at the level of good and bad, right and wrong, choices/behaviors/acts would lead us astray. Discernment is not the awareness of error; it is the envisioning of truth. The core of discernment is to be so filled with Godness, to be so in-Life that all that is illusion and non-Reality falls off like the ineffectual sham that it is. To know God is to see the universe as it is. To not be fooled or deluded. To be rooted and grounded in the heart of God. To live and have our being there. George Fox was one of the most discerning men of Christendom. His sensibilities were sharpened almost beyond what he could bear. But seeing the size and shape of death around him was not his place of empowerment. He could not rest until he finally saw the ocean of Light and the Love flow over the ocean of darkness. Then in the Truth of the realities of the universe, he had a place to stand. A place from which he could not be moved. He became a true discerner.

The early motions of discernment in a person are often cast in thoughts and perceptions: "something is wrong." Discerning persons grow up feeling that they are critical and judgmental. They are often deeply troubled by things that no one else seems to perceive. The good news is that the person is beginning to perceive *under*, to question the forgeries of the universe, to worry and be troubled that others are not perceiving the same realities. But I suspect that discernment is not mature and health-giving until one's vision is filled with the view of God, His nature, Her purposes, Their impact upon the present situation. The discerner must not only recognize the evil that would so easily beset us, but also be a fanatical and consistent envisioner and practitioner of redemption. That is the heart of God. For redemption is that motion of Life that moves into the eye of evil and explodes its arrangement from the inside out; freeing each element of the situation to be rearranged for Life.

If we were to bring to this discussion the basic notion that life-in-God is a process of being right—"righter" than the "lost"—we will view discernment as a vehicle for keeping us safe from being wrong or mistaken. If we see *EVIL* as a powerful enemy, we will demand of discernment the ability to keep us alert and informed of evil which is "out there to get us." If we have forgotten the lesson of Galatians, are living under our brand of legalisms to entitle us to God's favor, we will use discernment as a tool to keep ourselves and others "in line." We will use it to know who is "in" and who is "out." If discernment is perverted into sleuthing the evil in persons and in situations, it degenerates into judgment/criticism that is divorced from its fundamental function and nature-Love. All of these approaches will reduce discernment to a sword unto death rather than a scalpel unto Life. Only when discernment is knowing God does the truth of its function begin to emerge.

Characteristics of Discernment

Discernment is a perceptual ability.

Discernment is the ability to perceive good from evil. Its perceptions may come through a feeling, a knowing, or even a physical sensation. Inasmuch as there is an arrangement of life that is a counterfeit; and given that most of the world operates as if the counterfeit were the currency of the universe—discernment sees *under* and *through*. It senses from what spirit, from what source a thought or behavior is coming. It is that illumination that looks under the obvious to perceive what is truly operative. This becomes crucial to those who no longer walk by the Law, but by Grace. Under the Law, one clearly knew where one stood. There were objective yardsticks to see if all were going well. The Law of the Spirit appears to be more illusive to us. Things are not always as they seem. The surface does not always portray the heart. Jesus' recorded conversations are so often enigmatic because he was speaking with discernment to the internal realities rather than to the surface interactions. Jesus always spoke *under* to the core of the issue. And it certainly looked upside-down. The publican is commended for entering the Kingdom of God;

the Pharisee is about to be cast into perdition. So much that seemed to be "right" was challenged by the actions and teachings of Jesus. Jesus' discernment knew the heart. The heart of another. The heart of God.

Discernment is living, not simply perceiving.

The discerning person responds and makes choices that are consonant with his/her seeings. I believe that part of the greatness of Quakers has been that not only have they been a discerning people, but they understood that this was a living matter, not just an evaluation matter. Quakers have been quick to put their lives where their understandings were.

It is necessary to live into the fullness of one's Light and discernment even before we have the whole picture. It would be nice to wait until we see how everything fits together. But that is a luxury that we cannot wait for. What is required is that we walk in what we know now. In the walking, more will be added. In the obedience to the discernment we presently have, more discernment will be opened to us. I believe that is part of the meaning of what Jesus said: that to those who had, more would be given. And to those who had not, it would be taken from them. (Matthew 13:12) In refusing to act on what we already know, we become increasingly blind. If a person is using discernment to keep themselves and others safe from failure, this is a very difficult point to live out. The temptation is to be like the man in the parable that had one talent. He was afraid that he would do the wrong thing, so he took his talent and buried it so it would remain unrisked until he could return it to his master. To live in the partialness of our knowings is a necessary risk of walking in the Spirit.

Discernment is never the "end of the sentence."

We do not discern simply to know. Solomon asked God for a hearing heart to discern good from evil so that he might govern God's people well. (I Kings 3:9-12) This simple sentence is so rich in the knowledge of discernment! Solomon knew the truth about whose people it was that he was called to govern. How easy it would have been to take it at face value that this was his nation. He understood that discernment was rooted in being able to hear and obey God's voice. And he understood that discernment was not the end of the sentence. Discernment is always a service that is given in Love for others. It is to free, to heal, to call to Truth and Life. Its function is bathed and immersed in Love. Now this can be difficult. Discerning flirts with some of our most deadly failings: the way we use knowings for control, for one-upmanship that feeds our ego, for the idolatry of being our own gods. Some of us shiver when we hear and speak of discernment—for we have felt the sting of discernment that used a knowing to hurt and harm another. And did that in the name of God. Discernment's task is not completed with simply knowing; it needs to bridge to the reality of God's will being done on earth as it is in heaven.

Discernment is of the Spirit/spirit—God's Holy Spirit and our spirit.

Discernment is not logically derived. This is not at all to say that one ceases to think rationally and well. It is to say, however, that logic is not the judge of whether a discernment is of God or not. The mind becomes informed by the spirit, rather than the other way around. Discernment cannot be empirically judged; it is ultimately a faith statement. It is a gamble of faith. It is obedience to an inward monitor—and upon that we risk all. There is often no immediate indication of whether we are hearing and discerning or whether we are deluded by our own predispositions or we are crazy. After all, it could have been that Abraham was only responding to his deep wish to escape it all at Ur. Or that the pressure simply got too much for him and he began to see and hear things that weren't there. I know of no wonderful criteria by which we can know that we are truly hearing and responding to Truth and Goodness. There weren't any in Scripture. Consider Mary who spent at least thirty-four years out on a limb of believing the unbelievable. There was not a "three point check system" for her. She simply risked all unconditionally. Yes, we do have some checks and balances between our experiential knowings, our understandings of Scripture and the corporate listening of the community of faith. But ultimately we are left to both a personal and a corporate risk. I believe there is no way to get around it. Discernment, far from keeping us "safe," puts us at the outposts of our comfort zones. We choose to live into the fullness of our Light, regardless of the consequences. With Job we echo, "Even though he slay me, yet will I trust that it is God at work in me."

Discernment has only one Source—and all that is discerned is in alignment with the nature of that Source.

It should probably go without saying—but knowledge derived from spirits other than God's Spirit are inappropriate/unholy/unrighteous, and ultimately not life giving. The *ALL in ALL* is the fount of all of our knowing. We need no other. The narrative of the Fall would tell us that humankind has been faked out on this issue before.

Discernment sees the big redemptive picture.

The discerning person so knows God's intents of love and goodness, God's transformation of all weakness, tragedy, and shortcoming that the world is viewed in hope. No longer do we have to avert and avoid the weakness, insufficiency, unworthiness, even the cruelty in ourselves and others. There is a God that can take the worst of ourselves and others and weave it into a tapestry of glory, an alchemy of transformation. The discerning person sees—and therefore can become a co-partner of redemption upon the earth. To step with a willing heart into the middle of life's difficulties, and therefore to explore their sting and horror, is to be a transformer or Light and Life. Discernment not only sees through the sham, it sees into redemption and restoration.

Practical Guidelines for Discernment

So what are the practical guidelines in the matter of individual discernment? The questions that haunt us are: How can I know if I am hearing God? How can I ever tell what is discernment and what is my own internal material? What if I am wrong? What do I do when I see things quite differently from those around me?

My first observation is that discernment *is*. We don't ask for it, nor can we escape it. It is part of our perceptual field. When we turn our heart Godward, there is a reorientation to the universe that happens deep within our spirit. If we listen to the inner sense of reorganization, we begin to order our lives/make choices/live differently in accordance with that new internal sense. As we live out of our new orientation, our new perceptions, we become increasingly astute and wise, increasingly consonant. We walk in the Spirit. It is a natural growth process. What often happens to us, however, is that we do not attend to the new internal paradigm. We are not true to what rises within us. We deny, repress, live in contradiction to the new Life that is rising inside of us. It causes internal havoc. We are at war with ourselves. We are in confusion about our God. We suddenly find ourselves very unsure of what is real and what is not. Then the issue of discernment and guidance and listening becomes very difficult to know about. Interestingly enough, the more out of touch we are with ourselves and our God, the more tenaciously we cling to needing to know. We become desperate not to make mistakes. There is a very frantic quality in trying to find "God's will." We are not at ease with ourselves or our God, when, out of fear, we have chosen not to listen to our Inward Monitor, when we have been too afraid to risk the life of faith.

"But how do I know if it is God?" I hear folks cry agonizingly. I could tell you the standard replies. There is a "self-authenticating" quality to the voice of God within. The sheep know the voice of their shepherd. It is the lining up of all the factors until there is inward and outward consonance. God is recognized by the peace and at-homeness that follows. God is recognized by the movement towards increased love and adoration of the Godhead. One can know if one is following God if one observes the fruit of the Spirit accompanying the process. All of these thoughts are true. But in a sense, none satisfy the questioning heart. Again, I submit to you my own conviction: until the basic decision to risk all is made, no answer will satisfy. Once that decision has been made—all the above are useful, but none are really necessary.

You see, the issue is much less complicated than we make it. The life of faith is that we claim all of ourselves. The good, the bad; the wondrous and the despicable; the beautiful and the ugly; the whole and the broken; the light and the dark. We claim and take responsibility for our being—all of it. In the absolute realness of our entirety, we abandon ourselves into the Presence of God. There we abide. There we live forever. There we never try to "get ourselves together" and do life our own way again. There we do not fear ourselves and the darkness that is within us, for God's love has encompassed us with grace and mercy and given us Life. There we do not need to beat ourselves down with self-doubts and interrogations, for we are safe—just as we are. The road to many conversion experiences is paved with the words, "Just as I am." What we have not realized is that the Christian life is lived exactly as it was birthed—in the total reality of ourselves thrown upon the mercy of God.

Over and over I experience and observe that the great separations from knowing God come because you and I get out of the reality of ourselves. God wants to interact with us. Not someone else. Not a cleaned up version of ourselves. Not a dehumanized form of ourselves. Just us. It is from this place of being truly ourselves that we make the next choices for Life as they rise within us. We don't expect ourselves to become detached from ourselves and somehow participate in a "pure" Godness. We are not a sterile container through which God's thoughts flow. We don't expect ourselves to be totally right—when were we ever before? We simply offer up the reality and complexity of ourselves to God and to one another, and watch to see what transformations and redemptions are wrought. As we live this out, we find that the agony of expecting our discernment to be other-than-us evaporates like dew in the sun. Wonderful freedom is birthed.

"Well, what if we are deluded in this naive sort of state?" Well, what if we are? If God's transforming grace were enough to cover my sinfulness when I was rebellious, how much more there must be provision when my heart is eagerly leaping into His Presence and Heart. God's nature is faithful to who I am. God knows my limitations. God knows my uprisings and my downfallings. The Godhead will not leave me without a witness. God will send those occasions and persons of correction. Now I hear you say, "No, I don't want to have to be corrected! I want to do it right the first time!" The spirit of pride in us so quickly would move us from that place of trust and communication. Underneath that pride, however, is usually the terrible pain from our childhood that taught us that to be wrong or mistaken was to be unlovable and rejected. Our Lord calls us to a new resting place where there is freedom from the stress and strain of needing to be good, needing to be right, needing to achieve. There is no safer place in the universe than in the Presence of our loving and communicating God.

I am aware that coming to this place requires tender healing for many of us. It certainly has meant that for me. If healing is what we need, so be it. Meet Jesus experientially and let Him speak to your fragmented, frightened condition of being loved so poorly throughout your life. Some know their brokenness, while others have learned to cope by being strong and capable. When we do this, we can't even feel how frightened we are by the conditional love we have received. We only know that if we aren't in control and doing everything right, it feels as if we die. Let God's Spirit pierce the facade of that four-year-old trying to act like a brave soldier. And let the child know the release of being loved unconditionally by the heart of God. And if you know the healing of God and you have been lured out by our constant enemy, pride, release it. Drop it and return to the truth of yourself.

"Well, what if I do harm to another when I am wrong?" Of course, we will cause pain for another. Our very existence upon the earth means that we will be a cause of great blessing and pain for others. There is no way to avoid giving and receiving pain in this broken world. The very best we can give each other still has the "underbelly" of our own inadequacies and insufficiencies. I cannot be a perfect spouse, a perfect parent, a perfect friend, a perfect Christian—not even if I am centered and walking in the fullness of the Light. You and I are not perfect. We are promised that the brokenness of our lives can be transformed in Jesus Christ. This is not to deny that we are certainly in the process of becoming new creatures. For there is a wonderful miracle that happens as we stay abandoned in the Presence of God that indeed transforms our personhood. What I *do* hold up for question, however, is the prideful internal sense that swells within us, that secretly tells us that we are now "perfect." I question the horrible bondage that comes from that condition in which we try to make that perfection come to pass—expecting that to be the case if we are "truly committed."

But pain is not the end of the story. We are promised that pain need not be unto death—in our life or the life of another. Everyone always has the ability to choose pain-unto-Life. Our brokenness cannot damn another. It may cause great and grievous pain; but it can always be transformed and become the wondrous cause for rejoicing. (Genesis 50:19,20 Romans 8:28) Making a mess in life is humbling and painful, but it is not the end of the world. "But what if someone does make it the end of their world?" you respond. That is their choice. They had a choice to Live, just as you do. I believe that God's gracious mercy does not allow life that is beyond choice. In fact, we see in the Old Testament that when a civilization was beyond the ability to make choices for Life, God ended them. (E.g., Genesis 15:16).

The corollary to this thought is one that has given Quakers such astounding power. Where there is life, there is still God, there is still hope. God's Spirit abides in every person and is capable of being chosen, no matter how badly life's deck seems stacked against him/her. And thus into seemingly hopeless tragedy and cruelty, Quakers tromped, fanning the almost cold embers into a flame of Life.

What Do I Do with the Discernments I Have?

Be true to what is inside. Put weight on it. Live by it. Hold it with sufficient tentativeness to be open to other things. Yet hold it with sufficient tenacity to live it out until moved differently. Change that is of God's Spirit will come from the inside out.

Immerse yourself in the Presence of God. Practice the Presence. The only priority of life worth having is knowing God personally, intimately, experientially. Any other priority is not to see clearly the terrain of *Life*. When in a conflict situation, fill the space with Love and Light. Pay less attention to the dynamics of the conflict, the discernment perception, and center upon the Truth of God in that moment, to that person, to that situation. Stay in the space of Love. Don't be lured out of it!

Offer up what is in you to others. Offer it up in living. Offer it up in words. It is a gift, not a cudgel. Let it rest lightly. Release your discernment from your ego and your expectations. Flow as a stream that is useful to those who can take from you and in no way diminished by those who can't. Remember, your discernment cannot "save" anything or anyone. Discernment is, at best, only the illumination by which a person can make choices. God never takes the power of choice and responsibility from any person. God will not be a big scapegoat in the sky: "God made me do it." God lets us see what the choices and consequences are. The responsibility for discernment never releases a person or a group from the responsibility of choice.

The Motions of Discernment

In closing, I believe that discernment is not a sorting ability; rather it is a recognition and alignment task. To discern is to know God. To be so in union with God's nature and heart, that we feel as joined as the Old Testament sense of sexual knowing. The tender intimacy. The wondrous intercoursing. The release of abandonment, trust, vulnerability. The utter peace, contentment, smiles that saturate the being. The discerner is a lover, a lover who is ill at ease in any other space except God/Love/Reality/Life. All else falls short of the glory of God and is perceived for the shortfall it is.

The first motion of discernment is to come: to come with all one's inadequacies, insufficiencies, weakness, evil, blind spots, pain. To come to the Love, the Light. To there bathe in Mercy. To shed the heavy begrimed garments of condemnation, failure, control, alienation, brokenness. To splash in childlike abandon in Life. To abide in the eye of God's care and affection. To see *all* from this perspective. To view life and its intertwinings from the place of being met, loved, and wondrously cared for.

The second motion is to live in the sensitivity of a delicate radar that perceives the slightest, most subtle Godward blip. It is to see and affirm the movements of God in the universe. And from these affirmations of words and life, all Truth and non-truth takes its rightful course.

WRITTEN AND ORGANIZATIONAL RESOURCES

BIBLIOGRAPHY

Working in Groups

Center for Conflict Resolution. *Building United Judgment: A Handbook for Consensus Decision Making*. Madison, WI: Center for Conflict Resolution, 1981. A thorough review of methods for making consensus work as a decision making process for groups.

————. *A Manual for Group Facilitators*. Madison, WI: Center for Conflict Resolution, 1977. A clear guide for learning skills involved in group facilitation, including planning, problem-solving and helping groups reach their own goals.

Coover, Virginia, Ellen Deacon, Charles Esser and Christopher Moore. *Resource Manual for a Living Revolution*. Philadelphia: New Society Publishers, 1978. A classic sourcebook on group process and other skills useful to those involved in social change through nonviolence.

Gastil, John. *Democracy in Small Groups*. Philadelphia: New Society Publishers, 1993. Contains a helpful discussion of decision making in groups, and some excellent questions and exercises for groups seeking to understand themselves and become more democratic.

Shields, Katrina. *In the Tiger's Mouth: An Empowerment Guide for Social Action*. Philadelphia: New Society Publishers, 1994. A readable and practical manual for dealing with obstacles to individual and organizational effectiveness.

Starhawk. *Truth or Dare*. New York: Harper, 1987. A refreshing look at group process from a feminist, spiritual point of view. Starhawk's brilliant examination of the nature of power offers creative alternatives for positive change in our personal lives, our communities, and our world.

Community and the Bigger Picture

Macy, Joanna. *World As Lover, World as Self*. Berkeley, CA: Parallax Press, 1991. Teaches us to consider ourselves connected to the world and its creatures; provides inspiring stories and meditations.

————. *Despair and Personal Power in the Nuclear Age*. Philadelphia: New Society Publishers, 1983. A groundbreaking work for overcoming "psychic numbing," it provides a rich array of exercises for groups.

Peavey, Fran. *By Life's Grace: Musings on the Essence of Social Change*. Philadelphia: New Society Publishers, 1994. Essays, poems and letters, "a rich book for lean times."

————. *Heart Politics*. Philadelphia: New Society Publishers, 1986. Stories and visions of a new kind of politics infused with humanity and humor.

Shaffer, Carolyn R., and Kristin Anundsen. *Creating Community Anywhere: Finding Support and Connection in a Fragmented World.* New York: Tarcher/Perigree, 1993. A view of the many ways we create community, this book includes a very useful "starter kit" of tools for groups.

Whitmyer, Claude, ed. *In the Company of Others, Making Community in the Modern World.* New York: Tarcher/Perigree, 1993. A thought-provoking anthology about our need for community, and some of the satisfactions and difficulties involved in building community.

Communication and Conflict Resolution Skills

Cornelius, Helen, and Shoshana Faire. *Everyone Can Win, How to Resolve Conflict.* Sydney, Australia: Simon and Shuster, 1989. A very practical guide to learning skills involved in conflict resolution from a team that has trained many people in Australia and elsewhere.

Fisher, Roger, and William Ury. *Getting to Yes.* New York: Penguin, 1983. One of the first and most widely used books on conflict resolution, it has excellent descriptions of how to focus on issues rather than on personalities and how to create options that will satisfy both parties in a dispute.

Mindell, Arnold. *The Leader as Martial Artist.* San Francisco: Harper/Collins 1993. Contains excellent chapters on conflict resolution and "minority awareness."

Tannen, Deborah. *You Just Don't Understand.* New York: Ballentine, 1990. This book illuminates some of the differences in the ways men and women communicate.

Ury, William. *Getting Past NO.* New York: Bantam, 1993. A guide to the skills involved in negotiation.

Weeks, Dudley. *The Eight Essential Steps to Conflict Resolution: Preserving Relationships at Work, at Home and in the Community.* New York: Tarcher, 1992. A clear and practical method of resolving conflicts.

Clearness And Discernment

Farnham, Suzanna, et al. *Listening Hearts: Discerning Call in Community.* Ridgefield, CT: Morehouse Publishing, 1991.

French, Eileen. "Conducting a Clearness Meeting." London: *The Friend*, August 7, 1987.

Lacey, Paul A. *Leading and Being Led,* Wallingford, PA: Pendle Hill Pamphlet, No. 264 (1985).

Leavitt, Mary Lou, Helen Steven, and Mary Synott. "Meetings for Clearness." In *Meeting Needs: A Handbook for Quaker Groups and Meetings,* London: Quaker Home Service, 1992.

Loring, Patricia. *Spiritual Discernment: The Context and Goal of Clearness Committees.* Wallingford, PA: Pendle Hill Pamphlet, No. 305 (1992).

New England Yearly Meeting. "Committees of Concern or Clearness." *Living with Oneself and Others: Working Papers on Aspects of Family Life*, chapter 9. New England Yearly Meeting, 1985.

Palmer, Parker. "The Clearness Committee: A Way of Discernment." *Weavings*, July/August 1988, pp. 37-40.

Sinclair, Claire. "Clearness: An Address to Montana Gathering of Friends 1990." *Friends Bulletin*, April 1991.

Taylor, Thomas. "Clearness." London: *The Friend*, November 30, 1990.

Quaker Hill Conference Center. *Friends Consultation on Discernment*. Quaker Hill Conference Center, 1985 (Out of print, but available in some libraries.)

ORGANIZATIONAL RESOURCES

Organizations Promoting Diversity, Study Groups, and Conflict Resolution

Equity Institute is a national, nonprofit multicultural agency committed to reducing oppression and teaching appreciation and understanding of diversity. Equity Institute offers public workshops and training programs including Dismantling Racism, Dismantling Classism, Appreciating Diversity, Dismantling Sexism. For information, write to them at 6400 Hollis Street, Suite 15, Emeryville CA, 94608 or call (510) 658-4577.

The Study Circles Resource Center offers an information kit with in-depth information on what study circles are, detailed guidelines to assist in organizing, leading and participating in study circles, and curriculum guides for studying topics of interest to social change workers including health, economics, racism, and international security. They are located at Route 169, P.O. Box 203, Pomfret, CT 06258; (203) 928-2616.

National Institute for Dispute Resolution, 1901 L Street, NW, Suite 600, Washington, D.C. 20036; (202) 466-4764. An organization promoting education about dispute resolution and its use in courts and educational institutions. NIDR can provide assistance in finding local dispute resolution services. (More than 400 community justice centers exist nationwide).

Organizations Promoting Support Groups For Members

The Impact Project is a nonprofit organization which organizes support groups for people with financial surplus (earned or inherited) who are seeking a more just and sustainable world. In addition, they offer individual counseling, workshops, a money workbook, and a quarterly newsletter ("More than Money"). Their work assists people to clarify their values around money, to take charge of their spending and investments, to deal better with money in their relationships, to create meaningful work, and to use their resources effectively to help make the world a better place. The Impact Project can be reached at 21 Linwood St., Arlington, MA 02174; (617) 648-0776. (Note: They are not a funding agency. Please do not contact them for referral to individual funders.)

Interhelp is an international network of people who share their deepest responses to world conditions that threaten human life and the earth. They help people within their own communities to move through feelings of isolation and hopelessness to empowerment. Interhelp offers community gatherings and training in Despair and Empowerment, Deep Ecology and personal support systems. Contact Interhelp at P.O. Box 86, Cambridge, MA 02140.

The Traprock Peace Center, a peace education center in Western Massachusetts, creates affinity groups for volunteers who assist the center. The groups foster a sense of mutual support while doing the work. For information contact the Traprock Peace Center, Woolman Hill, Keets Road, Deerfield, MA 01342; (413) 773-7507.

NEW SOCIETY PUBLISHERS

New Society Publishers is a not-for-profit, worker-controlled publishing house. We are proud to be the only publishing house in the United States committed to fundamental social change through nonviolent action.

We are connected to a growing worldwide network of peace, feminist, religious, environmental, and human rights activists, of which we are an active part. We are proud to offer powerful nonviolent alternatives to the harsh and violent industrial and social systems in which we all participate. And we deeply appreciate that so many of you continue to look to us for resources in these challenging and promising times.

New Society Publishers is a project of the New Society Educational Foundation and the Catalyst Education Society. We are not the subsidiary of any transnational corporation; we are not beholden to any other organization; and we have neither stockholders nor owners in any traditional business sense. We hold this publishing house in trust for you, our readers and supporters, and we appreciate your contributions and feedback.

New Society Publishers
4527 Springfield Avenue
Philadelphia, Pennsylvania
19143

New Society Publishers
P.O. Box 189
Gabriola Island, British Columbia
V0R 1X0